TCL VoicePro Installation and Programming the VP206 & VP412

For Software Version 2.021

Copyright © 2013, Stok Software, Inc.

VP206

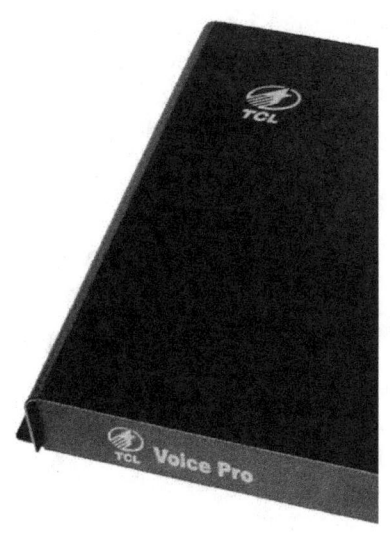

VP412

**TCL VoicePro Installation and
Programming the VP206 & VP412**

Copyright © 2013 Stok Software, Inc.

This manual is written for VoicePro Software Version 2.021.

The information contained in this manual is subject to change without notice.

Table of Contents

How to Use this Manual

This is the most up-to-date Installation and Programming Manual written by Stok Software for the new VoicePro manufactured by TCL.

Make use of everything in this manual to achieve the best user experience. To start with, the section "Know Your VoicePro" on page 15 covers all the parts and usage requirements.

"Installing Your VoicePro System" on page 19 discusses proper connection to phone lines and extension phones. It also explains how to do a "First Time Power Up" on page 29.

"Quick Start Programming" on page 33 involves programming steps necessary to have the VoicePro serve your most important needs.

"Auto Attendant Programming" on page 43 will help complete the picture with designing a front end to guide your callers.

In addition to system setup, "Programming Your Extensions" on page 51 covers details of setting up each extension for you personnel.

You will find yourself referencing the "Guide to Programming Functions" on page 61 often as this fully describes each program function.

Your personnel can make good use of "Using Your VoicePro System" on page 97 for details of all phone system features and usage. It also explains how to access and program their voice mailboxes.

About Stok Software, Inc.

In October 2010 Stok Software acquired the Distributorship of the new VoicePro manufactured by TCL Communication. You can now come to us for maintenance and support of your VoicePro products. .

Stok Software has had a unique start in the early 1980's by having shared in the development of software for home computers when the IBM PC was first announced. Stok Software developed the hard disk backup procedure that has become part of Concurrent PC-DOS. And as pioneers in the Voice Mail programming field, Stok had written the first Speech Editor (VBASE/40) for Dialogic Corporation (now owned by Intel). Stok Software designed the file structure for handling multi-prompt speech files which has become an industry standard used by Dialogic, Intel, Expert Systems, Compass Technology, Pika Technologies, Bitworks, Bicom, Cascade Technologies, and Voice Information Systems.

Developing Voice Mail Software in the 1980's has led Stok Software to continue their focus on offering many creative Telephone Communications solutions for small and large businesses. Stok's partnerships with providers, along with their own programming expertise and problem solving skills, have combined their energies to provide cost effective telecommunications and value-added services.

Stok Software used their expertise with software programming and documentation to write this more accurate and improved User's Manual for the VoicePro.

In addition to this manual, there's a lot of information to help you with the VoicePro on our web site. We can help you with your other personal and business communications needs as well. Visit us at...

www.stok.com

VoicePro Introduction

Please read all sections of this manual carefully to become familiar with all functions of your VoicePro. You will appreciate its value and features with proper installation and programming, which will greatly enhance its usefulness and operation.

The VoicePro is a professional-quality telephone system that works with your existing standard telephones and enhances their capability with calling features such as call transfer, call parking, busy transfer, call forwarding to cell phones, voice mail, message notification by message light or by voice, and much more.

You can record your own company greeting (Day, Night, and Weekend Greetings by your programmed schedule) and easily configure the VoicePro from any touch-tone phone. You can program a menu of choices to give your callers quick access to extensions or recorded information.

Provide your personnel with their own extensions with voice mail that can be picked up from any phone. The programmable menu options or extensions can ring in-house or forward anywhere.

The VoicePro answers your calls with your custom company greeting and prompts. It transfers callers to any extension or mailbox. It can even transfer callers to your cell phone or another location with its follow-me feature! With call screening, you can press a key to accept a call or send the caller to voicemail, which plays your personal mailbox greeting and takes a message.

The VoicePro is 100% electronic and has no moving parts or hard drive that can wear out. All recorded greetings and messages are stored on internal digital memory that can be upgraded to allow storage up to eight hours. Standard configuration includes two hours of voice storage.

There are two sizes of the VoicePro as outlined in this table.

VoicePro Model	Max Phone Lines	Max Extensions	Voice Mailboxes	Physical Extension numbers	Msg Space (hours)
VP206	2	6	99	10 thru 15	2, 4, or 8
VP412	4	12	99	10 thru 21	2, 4, or 8

All physical extensions (listed in above table) can re-route calls to outside phone numbers. All others can be used as voice mail only. Mailboxes range from 01 up to 99.

Each extension jack provides 24V DC power and ringing at 20Hz with 80V RMS and 0.4 Amps to support standard single-line telephones and fax machines.

VP206

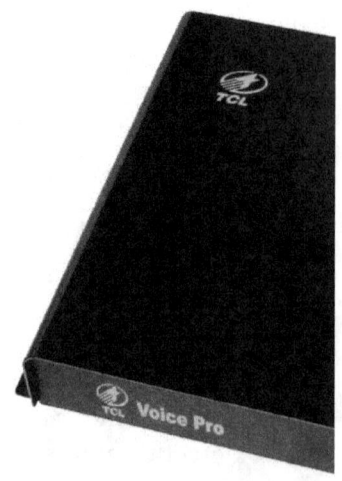

VP412

With simple programming, you can control all the features of the VoicePro, such as…

- Define Automated Attendant Menu Keys
- Set up Voice Mail for each extension
- Program Call Forwarding to cell phones or other numbers
- Select Message Waiting Light or stutter dial-tone
- Enable Live Message Notification
- Enable Call Screening
- Route Fax calls to your fax machine

System programming is done via any touch-tone telephone. Only you or people you designate as system administrator and who know the System Password are able to change the programming or operation of the system.

The system administrator can change individual mailbox passwords, change the system time, record or change system greetings, and program Auto Attendant applications. The system administrator can easily check for messages system wide so there is no need to log into each mailbox to find which mailboxes have messages.

The Automated Attendant assists with routing calls 24 hours a day by offering menu options (Press 1 for this, press 2 for that). You can create your own custom Auto Attendant menu with different Day, Night and Weekend Greetings. Calls can be routed to an extension, to a mailbox, to an outside number, to an informational announcement or a name directory.

The Automated Attendant also allows callers to dial known extensions directly. And each extension has its own personalized voice mail to take messages when the extension doesn't answer. Extensions may even be programmed to route calls to outside phone numbers such as cell phones.

Here is an example of a menu you can create...

> Thank you for calling XYZ Corp.
> If you know the extension you wish to reach, you may enter it at any time.
> For assistance, press 0.
> For Sales, press 1.
> For Technical Support, press 2.
> For Accounting, press 3.
> To listen to a description of our products, press 4.
> To hear directions to our office, press 5.
> For a company directory, press 9.

The internal clock controls how the system greets incoming callers by playing the appropriate greeting. You can record individual Day, Night and Weekend System Greetings. You can even customize greetings for each incoming phone line.

You can make the following Programming Assignments for your individual requirements...

- Record up to 99 greetings and assign to incoming lines.
- Assign other greetings for day, night and weekend modes.
- Use other greetings for voice-on-demand menu options.
- Assign incoming lines to ring to specific extensions.
- Specify the outgoing lines permissible for each extension.

You can specify which Call Forwarding Method works best in your installation for transferring calls...

- Two-line conference with supervised transfer.
- Three-way-calling... The VoicePro conferences the parties.
- Centrex... The VoicePro will release and free up the line.
- Two-line conference with blind transfer.

Note: In addition to this user manual, you can find additional information for programming and using your VoicePro online at www.stok.com/voicepro.html

Know Your VoicePro

Before installing your VoicePro system, it's important to read this manual without skipping sections so you know how to properly connect and program your system. You also need to be sure to have the proper phone company services active and tested.

About the Included Phone Wires and Splitters

The VP206 includes two long phone wires and two short six-inch wires. It also includes two splitter jacks. The VP412 doubles up on all the cables since it supports four phone lines.

The short wires are to be used with the splitters in case you need them. You'll only need to use the splitters if you have a single jack on the wall that has two phone lines. This is known as an RJ-14 jack.

If you have individual jacks for each phone line, then you don't need the splitters. Single-line jacks are known as RJ-11.

The line jacks and extension jacks on the back of the VoicePro are all single-line jacks.

If your phone service comes in with two lines in one jack, you need to use a splitter to divide two lines from and RJ-14 jack into two individual RJ-11 lines.

The Line Splitters Explained

There are two types of splitters included:

- A **Phone Line Splitter (Male-Female)** may be used if you have your incoming line service terminated with a two-line RJ-14 jack. Plug the Splitter into the RJ-14 jack and the other end gives you two separate single-line RJ-11 jacks. Plug two regular phone-line cords into these jacks and into the "Line" ports on the VoicePro.

- A **Two-line Coupler (Female-Female)** may be used if you want to connect a two-line phone to two extension ports. If the phone has only one "L1+L2" jack on the back, then you need a Coupler. Plug two short line cords into the jacks on one side of the coupler and into any two individual extension ports on the back of the VoicePro. Never connect two phones to the same extension port. Plug a long RJ-14 cable into the other side of the coupler and into the jack marked "L1+L2" on the phone. If you have a four-line phone, you can do the same thing for the next two lines, giving the phone four extension numbers. There is really no purposeful reason for doing this, because the VoicePro gives a single-line phone access to all outside lines anyway.

Power Adapter

The Power Adapter provided as standard equipment with your VoicePro is a 120VAC 60Hz, 24-Watt Class 2 Transformer providing output of 28VDC 600mA. It is strongly advised that you install a surge protector for the VoicePro. This will protect the system from a sudden increase in voltage (such as during a thunderstorm). Get something decent with a good warranty that covers loss of equipment due to power surges.

Battery Backup

The VoicePro contains a Maintenance-Free rechargeable Lead-Acid battery (6 Volt DC, 1.2 Amp Hour). This battery provides backup power to retain system programming, greetings and messages for up to five hours in the event of a power loss.

The battery does not supply ring-voltage. So the VoicePro will not take new messages while on battery power. During power outages it will pass incoming calls direct to extensions. Line 1 to extension 10, line 2 to extension 11, and so on. If you want full system functions during a power failure then connect the VoicePro to an uninterruptible power source (UPS).

What Phones Are Compatible?

The VoicePro supports 6 or 12 extensions (based on model) and uses standard phones that are not included. Multi-line phones are not necessary since the VoicePro gives multi-line access to a standard single-line phone. It also enhances any standard phone with all the features of larger corporate phone systems.

When you're selecting phones to use with the VoicePro, make sure they work on regular phone company jacks. Then you can be sure they will work with the VoicePro. Proprietary digital phones specific to other vendor's phone systems will not work and can damage the VoicePro.

You can find a list of recommended phones sets online at www.stok.com/standard-phone-sets.html

Message Waiting Light

If you want a message waiting light, make sure your phone uses a 90V message light. See page 82 for programming message waiting.

Phone Company Services You May Need

Caller ID: The VoicePro will pass the name and number to the individual extensions if you have Caller ID service on your phone lines.

Line Hunt/Rollover: This is recommended so that a busy line will roll over to the next line. This is the only way the VoicePro will be able to receive and handle multiple calls coming in on the same number. All the lines in the Hunt/Rollover Group should be connected to VoicePro.

How to Add Music on Hold

A radio, MP3 player, or other music source can be connected to the VoicePro to provide music to callers while on-hold and while being transferred. Use a 3.5 mm mono phono plug to connect your music source to the music jack on the rear of the VoicePro. See "Installing An External Music Source" on page 29 for installation details.

Memory Upgrade

Standard VoicePro units include two hours of message space. This can be increased to four or eight hours. You can replace the two 1-hour chips with one or two 4-hour chips. **Note that you will void the warranty if you open the unit.**

Unplug the red/black battery wires before changing the chips. When installing a single 4-hour chip, place it in the slot closest to the LED's. Leave the other slot unused. Leaving a 1-hour module in the other slot will cause errors.

When powering up the first time, extension 10 will ring a number of times to indicate how much memory is installed, as explained on page 31 in this manual. At any time you can use program function 93 to check how much total storage space is installed.

Installing Your VoicePro System

Read Before Connecting Your VoicePro

Please read this entire section BEFORE applying power.

Installation procedures and programming are the same for the VP206 or the VP412. The only difference is… The VP206 supports two CO (Phone Company Central Office) lines and six extensions. The VP412 supports four CO lines and 12 extensions.

All jacks on the back of the unit are RJ-11. This means they each handle one line and can be connected directly to the CO line jack on the wall. The image at the right shows how a VP206 is connected to two RJ-11 CO jacks. With the VP412 you can attach up to four CO lines.

The extension jacks are also RJ-11 and each jack should be used for a single-line phone. See the discussion on "Using Two-line and Four-line phones" on page 24.

Important!!!
DO NOT connect any CO lines to extension ports.
This will cause permanent damage to the system.

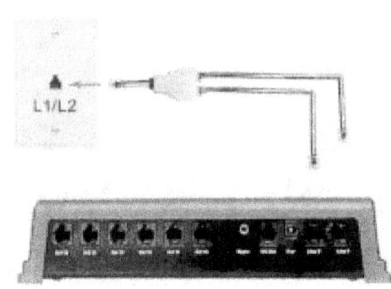

If you have the CO lines coming in on RJ-14 jacks (two lines in one jack) then you will need to use the included line splitter. This splits an RJ-14 two-line jack into two RJ-11 single lines. These single lines then connect to the CO Line jacks on the back of the VoicePro as shown in the image at the left. The line splitter is included and is also available from Radio Shack (ask for part number 279-401).

Make sure you use the correct line splitter. A common mistake is using a splitter that looks the same but one that splits a two-line RJ-14 into two RJ-14 rather than dividing the lines into two single lines (RJ-11). Splitting the wrong way may cause two CO ports to be shorted together and cause erroneous processing. Test your split by first connecting a phone to one of the split lines and make test calls to and from that phone. Then test the other split line the same way. Don't connect to the VoicePro until you are sure you have the individual CO lines terminating as individual RJ-11 wires.

You can complete the connections to your VoicePro by following these steps:

1. Connect the telephone company lines to the "Line" jacks on the rear of your VoicePro unit.
2. Connect your telephone sets to the extension ports.
3. Connect the power supply to your unit.
4. Connect an external music source for music-on-hold if desired.

Detailed installation procedures are covered on the following pages.

Connecting Telephone Company CO lines

The VoicePro has standard RJ-11 jacks on the back labeled "Line 1" and up. Connect your Telephone Company Central Office (CO) lines to these jacks as shown below.

VP206 Configuration

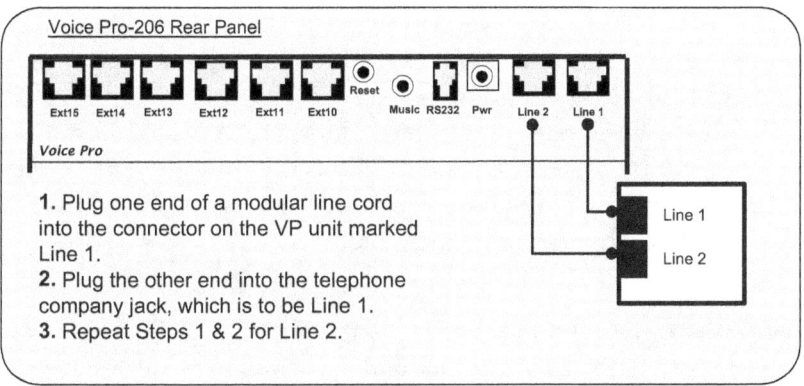

VP412 Configuration

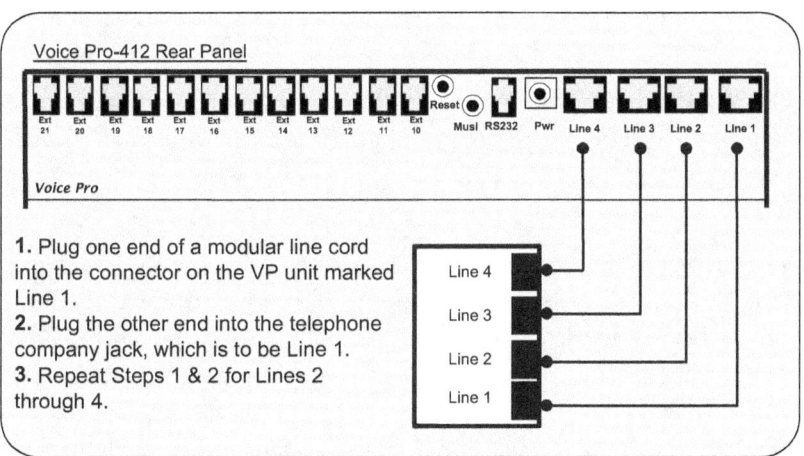

Safety Tip: Phone wires carry only a very slight charge, but ringing voltage can shock you. Disconnect the main feed line at your demarcation box or Network Interface Device when working on phone wiring. Avoid working on phone wiring if you have a pacemaker, or if there's an electrical storm. Be aware of any electrical lines if you are cutting into a wall or snaking phone cable.

Important: The CO lines connected to the VoicePro must be dedicated to servicing the unit. Do not connect any other phones or equipment to these lines. If you have a security system that requires an outside phone line, that system needs its own dedicated line. Do not allow a security system to share the same phone line with the VoicePro. Any other equipment sharing the same lines may cause conflicts with the operation of the VoicePro.

Warning: DO NOT connect a telephone CO line to a station extension port. This will cause permanent damage to your unit.

Warning: When connecting the extension stations to the VoicePro, make sure that the 2nd pair (black and yellow wires) on the RJ11 jack is isolated. DO NOT connect a telephone or any other device to this pair to avoid damage to the system.

Warning: Do not connect multiple phones to a single VoicePro extension port. The ring-voltage is sufficient for only one phone per extension port.

Warning: Do not use proprietary phones from other phone systems that are not standard analog phones. Connecting a digital phone to the VoicePro can cause permanent damage and void your warranty.

Note: The RS-232 jack is reserved for factory use only and is not available for any end-user function.

Wiring Extensions

All the extension ports on the VoicePro use single-line connections known as RJ-11 and should be connected to a single-line phone. Using multi-line phones is not necessary since the VoicePro provides access to all lines with a standard single-line phone. This is discussed in the next section below.

You need to run standard twisted-pair telephone cables from each location where you want to have a telephone extension. Typical telephone cable has four conductors. When you open the wall jacks you should find a mounting plate with four screw terminals labeled R, G, B, and Y (red, green, black, and yellow). The jacks will also have 2 or 4 individual wires that run from the screw terminals to the modular jack.

You will only use the red and green wires for one line from each extension. All the cables should run to the place where you have your VoicePro. To connect to the VoicePro you should have RJ-11 Modular plugs on the end of the cables. It is recommended that all your distant extensions and the CO lines terminate with RJ-11 wall jacks. Line them up on the wall. Then use standard telephone wires with RJ-11 plugs on each end to connect the jacks to the VoicePro. This makes it easy to switch connections if you want to change one physical extension to another.

Reusing Existing Lines

If you place your VoicePro at the Demarcation Location, you will save a lot of headaches rewiring an old phone system. This is where all the lines come together and connect to the outside phone line. You may find this on the side of your building or in the basement. It may be a punch-down block or a Network Interface, which looks similar to a wall jack. This is the legal demarcation point where the outside wiring from the street (owned by the telephone company) meets the wiring inside your house (owned by you).

Since all the lines from the premises come to the Demarcation Location, you may be able to salvage your existing lines, which presently may all be wired together if you had all your phones on the same line. What you need to do is separate all the lines at the Demarcation Location, and attach an RJ-11 Modular Jack to each line so they can be plugged into the respective extension ports on the VoicePro. The trick is to know which line goes to which telephone extension. Well, once you are done with the wiring, and assuming you did it right, you can call each extension from another to find out which phone is ringing. Then make adjustments as desired by changing connections on the unit itself.

Important: You must configure your wiring with a direct path from each phone extension to the VoicePro. In residential construction, "loop-through" wiring is more common, where the circuit passes from one jack to another and another. If this is the case, you can change some of the connections to reconfigure one or more jacks with a direct path. But you may be forced to run additional new cables to make direct paths for all the extensions.

Cat-3 and Cat-5 Cable

If you are in a newer building or one where new telephone cable has been installed, you may encounter "Cat-3" or "Cat-5" cable. These both contain four pairs of wires, enough for four separate phone lines. The pairs for a single line are usually twisted together. They consist of a solid-color wire with a white spiral, and a white wire with a spiral that matches the solid color of that pair.

Using Two-line and Four-line Phones

There is really no purposeful reason for using a multi-line phone with the VoicePro, because it gives a single-line phone access to all outside lines anyway. But if you want to use two-line phones, and assign two extensions to that phone, you will need to use a line coupler.

Plug two short line cords into the jacks on one side of the coupler and into any two individual extension ports on the back of the VoicePro. Never connect two phones to the same extension port. Plug a long RJ-14 cable into the other side of the coupler and into the jack marked "L1+L2" on the phone. If you have a four-line phone, you can do the same thing for the next two lines, giving the phone four extension numbers.

⚡ **Warning:** Don't use non-twisted "quad" cable, as this will probably introduce some crosstalk. You may hear the conversation on the other line at a very low level. Use only twisted-pair wire to avoid crosstalk.

Equipment Connections

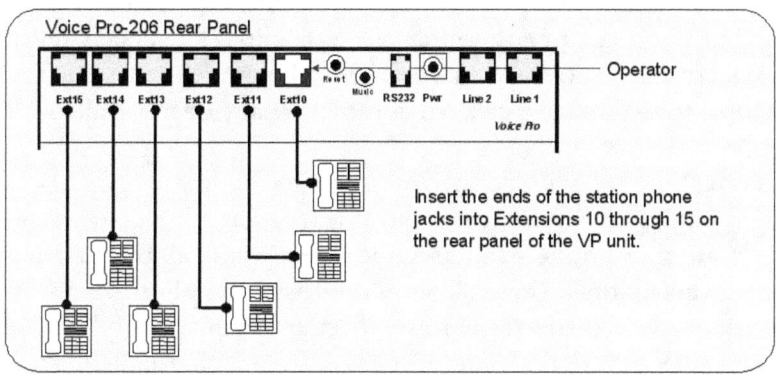

Important: If you use cordless phones for your extensions they may interfere with one another. Make sure each cordless handset and its base use unique codes. And also make sure users don't place the handsets into the wrong base units. If you start having strange things happen they may have been hung up on the wrong base.

⚡ **Warning:** Do not connect multiple phones to a single VoicePro extension. Ring-voltage is sufficient for only one phone per extension.

25

Test All Lines Before Using the VoicePro

Before you complete the installation of your VoicePro it is extremely important to test all your lines first by making various calls with the phones connected but NOT using the VoicePro yet. This will help avoid frustration later in case you find that things are not working as expected. This is often a result of the phone lines wired wrong or the necessary phone services not having been enabled.

The first step is to check that your Caller-ID is working. Connect a phone that had a Caller-ID display to your first CO line and call that number from another phone. Make sure it displays correctly. Do the same test with each line.

The second step is to test the proper functioning of rollover from a busy line to the next line. You need Line Hunt/Rollover service from your phone company so that the VoicePro can actually receive all the calls coming in to the first line. This allows using just one number for people to dial but the call can come in on any of the available lines.

To test the rollover, connect a phone to the first line and call from another phone. It should ring. Now leave that phone off-hook and connect another phone to the second line. Again call the first number from another phone. That call should ring on the phone connected to the second line if it rolled-over as expected. If not, notify your phone company. Continue the same test for all remaining lines if you have more than two. The VP206 can only handle two lines but the VP412 supports up to four incoming lines.

The third test is necessary only if you plan to have VoicePro extensions forward calls to outside numbers. Using just a phone connected to the line, try manually forwarding an incoming test-call by doing a hook-flash (press the flash key) and dial another number. If you plan to let the VoicePro free up the line make sure that works by hanging up after the transfer and check to be sure the two parties did not lose each other. You will need this service from the phone company in order to release the line to be available for other callers.

26

Connecting a Fax Machine

You can connect a fax machine to any one of the extension jacks. If automatic Fax Detection is desired, you need to program the VoicePro to route fax calls to the extension where you have your fax machine (see Program Function 7) and you need to enable fax detection on the desired CO lines (see Program Function 31).

When Fax Detection is enabled, the VoicePro delays answering incoming calls a few seconds to detect a fax CNG signal. If no CNG is received the VoicePro will handle the call as a regular voice call.

Using VoIP Phone Lines (Phone via Internet)

When you pick up a station extension to make a call, you get outside dialtone from any available line. Some VoIP telephone adapters do not provide dialtone with proper voltage and the VoicePro will assume this is a dead CO line.

If you use a VoIP line and you have problems finding an available line to make outbound calls, dropping calls during a conversation, echo during conversations, or failure to answer incoming calls, your VoIP adapter may not be compatible.

We continually discover models that work and models that are incompatible. See "VoIP Compatibility Issues" on our website for a complete up-to-date list. The following are a few adapters that were tested and passed.

- Motorola Model VT1005V Voice Terminal
- Motorola Model SBV5120 broadband modem
- Motorola Model SBV5322 4-Line SURFboard®
- RCA Model DHG535
- Cisco Model DPC2203C
- Vonage® V-Portal™ Phone Adapter (Model VDV21-VD)

27

Installing The Power Adapter

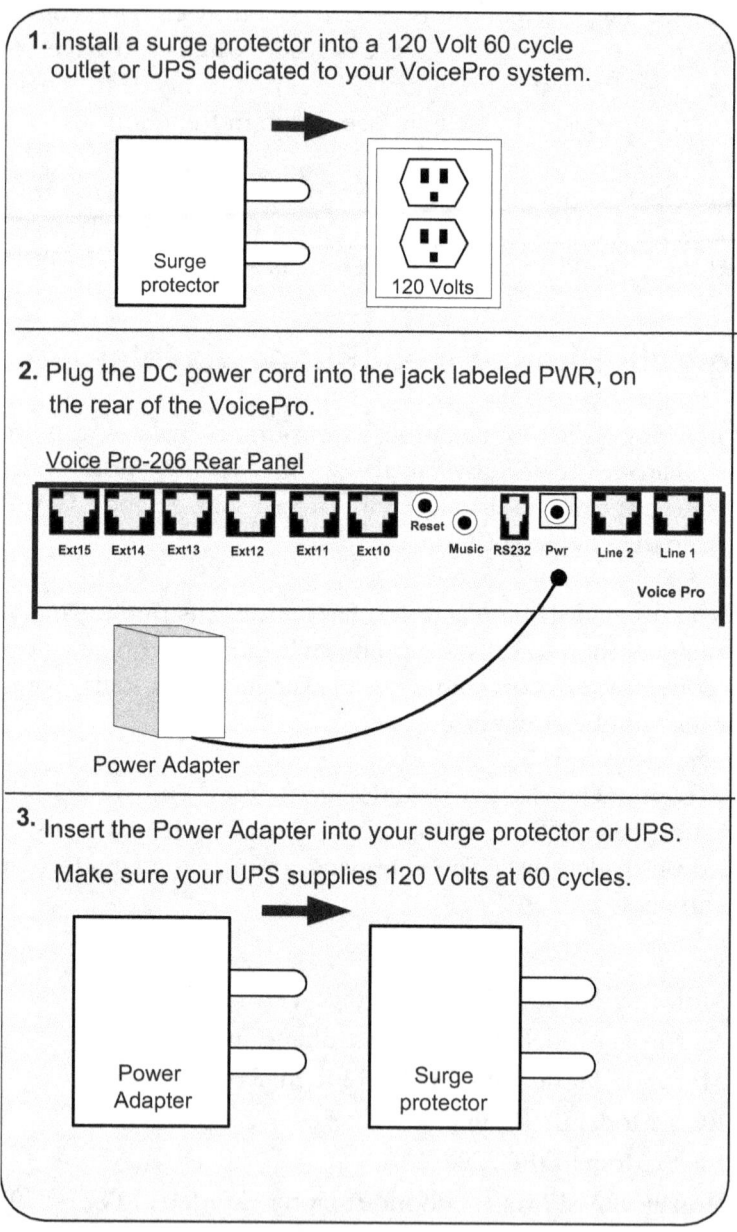

1. Install a surge protector into a 120 Volt 60 cycle outlet or UPS dedicated to your VoicePro system.

Surge protector

120 Volts

2. Plug the DC power cord into the jack labeled PWR, on the rear of the VoicePro.

Voice Pro-206 Rear Panel

Ext15   Ext14   Ext13   Ext12   Ext11   Ext10   Reset   Music RS232 Pwr   Line 2   Line 1

Voice Pro

Power Adapter

3. Insert the Power Adapter into your surge protector or UPS.

Make sure your UPS supplies 120 Volts at 60 cycles.

Power Adapter

Surge protector

First Time Power Up

Make sure you have a phone connected to extension 10. The VoicePro will run a system check the first time. **Extension 10 will ring a number of times to indicate how much memory is installed...** Two rings if 2 hours are available, three rings if 4 hours are available, and four rings if 8 hours are available.

Do not operate the unit during system startup, which can take anywhere from one to three minutes.

The yellow FULL light will slowly flash on and off while the system is running through its testing mode.

When the system startup is successful and the VoicePro is ready for use, extension 10 will ring six more times and the yellow FULL light will stop flashing.

The red PWR light will remain on, indicating the unit is ready.

Note: If power fails or is disconnected from the VoicePro unit, the yellow FULL light will flash to indicate that it is running on battery power. This will continue until battery power is exhausted, or power is restored.

If the internal battery has been preserving the system memory during a power failure, extension 10 will *not* ring as noted above to indicate how much memory is found available on startup. This is only done when booting the system the first time.

When power is restored after a power failure extension 10 will ring only one time to indicate that power has been restored.

You can always check how much memory is installed by using Program Function 93. Program Functions will be discussed later.

Status Indicator Lights

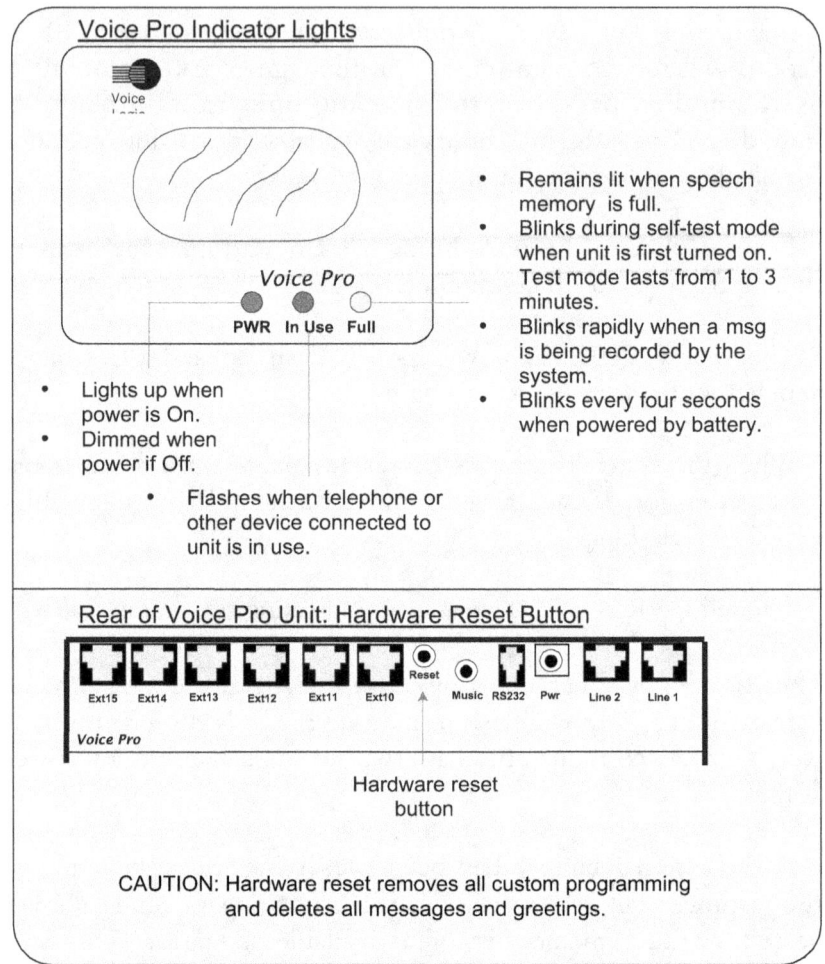

Note: The above display shows the VP206. The VP412 has similar Indicator Lights and connections.

The Hardware reset button reboots the system processor, deletes all voice mail messages and greetings, therefore freeing all memory, resets all program functions to their default states, including the time and date.

Attaching a Music-on-Hold Device

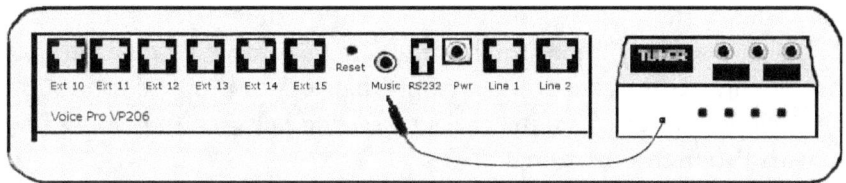

Plug the supplied 3.5 mm mono phono plug into the music jack on the real of the VoicePro. Connect the other end into a headphone jack on your music source. To avoid interference, plug the music source into a different outlet other than the one for the VoicePro.

The output from your music source needs to be about 0.7v. Check the user's manual of the device you are using for your on-hold source to be sure it has the proper signal strength. It should be the standard output that is used for headphones.

The on-hold volume level is adjusted from the external device. Program function 41 is only used to adjust the volume of the prompts, greetings and voice mail messages. It does not control the volume of your on-hold, which is dependant on the signal strength from your music-on-hold device.

Make sure you are using a mono output. If you are using a stereo output, you will only be feeding one channel to the VoicePro. Many radios have a mono switch which combine the two channels into one. If you are using a CD with a custom on-hold recording, it may only have been recorded on one track. If you use a stereo connection feeding the other track, you will have little or no volume at all. Setting your device to mono mode will correct this problem.

Warning: <u>DO NOT</u> plug the music source into an extension port. This will cause permanent damage to your unit and may void the warranty.

Volume Controls

The system volume, for both greetings and voice mail messages, can be adjusted in case you later find that it is too low or too loud for your telephone sets. You may select a setting between the ranges of 15-32 with Program Function 41.

It is also possible to increase or decrease the volume while listening to a voicemail message from your mailbox by pressing 7 repetitively to decrease the playback volume, or 9 repetitively to increase the playback volume. This temporary adjustment will stay in effect until you leave your mailbox or hang up.

Quick Start Programming

This section will get you started quickly with programming the essentials. The following section (Pg 43) discusses programming your Auto Attendant Menu. The section after that (Pg 51) involves the details on programming your extensions. After that is a complete guide to all the programming functions (Pg 61).

Default Passwords...

When entering passwords, you need to press the # key when done. Passwords are preset to the following defaults:

- System Password for Program Mode: 1234

- Regular full-featured mailboxes: 4321

- Greeting-only mailboxes: **99

Important: Remember the new System Password you specify. The only recourse if you forget this password is to reset the entire system back to factory default with the reset button on the back. All greetings and messages will be lost and all factory defaults will be reset.

Important Tip: It is suggested that you write out your programming plan on paper, step by step, when you do it the first time. By doing that, you'll have an easy-to-follow list in case you need to redo the programming in the future, rather than doing it from scratch.

Note: Regular mailboxes are those that are assigned to physical extensions. The default password is 4321. All other mailboxes default as Greeting-Only mailboxes. They only play their greeting announcement. Their default password is **99. You can change any Greeting-Only mailbox to a regular mailbox by changing the password to one that does not start with a star.

Tip: Individual mailbox passwords can be reset with Program Function 26. If you changed the status of a mailbox, it will remain that way and the default password will be set accordingly. Regular mailboxes are reset to 4321 and Greeting-Only mailboxes are reset to **99.

Accessing Programming Mode

You will need to enter programming mode to carry out any of the programming tasks. Pick up any extension and press the # key. If the Automated Attendant is enabled, you can also enter programming mode remotely. Just call any line connected to your VoicePro and press the # key when it answers.

The system will announce the date and time and say, "Welcome to VoicePro. Please enter your password followed by the pound."

Note: If you hear it say, "Welcome to station programming" then you did not enter the system programming mode. This can occur if you don't have the unit attached to outside lines. You can force it into Programming Mode by pressing the # key quickly after you pick up. Don't wait for the "Welcome to VoicePro" prompt, just pick up and press # before the unit has a chance to determine if it found a live line.

Once you hear the prompt for the System Password, enter it followed with the # key. The default is 1234#. The system will say, "Password accepted. Please press the desired program number followed by the pound". Now you can enter any of the Program

Function codes. You may exit program mode at any time by pressing the star key twice (* *).

Note: After three incorrect password attempts you will be rejected from the system.

Note: While in programming mode, if you do not make an entry within one minute after the prompt, the system will hang up. All programming done to that point will be saved.

Specify Telephone Lines Installed

It is important to tell your VoicePro which lines are connected. If you are using less that two lines on the VP206 or less than four lines with the VP412 then you need to specify which lines are connected. If you don't specify this, the VoicePro may have delays providing dial tone when you pick up an extension. This is because it may search on lines that are not connected. You can avoid this delay by locking out the lines that are not connected.

1. Enter Programming Mode.
2. Enter Program Function 2# (Telephone Lines Installed).
3. When prompted, enter *all* the lines you have attached to active Central Office (CO) lines. Then press #.
   - If one line is installed, press 1#.
   - If two lines are installed, press 12#.
   - If three lines are installed, press 123#.
   - If four lines are installed, press 1234#.
4. Press * * to end programming and hang up.

Set the Time

1. Enter Programming Mode.
2. Enter Program Function 19# (Time Set).
3. When prompted, enter the hour (1 thru12), then press #.
4. When prompted, enter the minutes (00 thru 59), then press #.
5. When prompted, enter 1# for AM or 2# for PM.
6. Press * * to end programming and hang up.

Set the Date

1. Enter Programming Mode.
2. Enter Program Function 20# (Date Set).
3. When prompted, enter the month (1 thru 12), then press #.
4. When prompted, enter the day (1 thru 31) and then press #.
5. When prompted, enter the year and then press # (enter as "13#" for 2013).
6. When prompted, enter the day of the week from the table below, then press #.

   1 = Monday
   2 = Tuesday
   3 = Wednesday
   4 = Thursday
   5 = Friday
   6 = Saturday
   7 = Sunday

7. Press * * to end programming and hang up.

Call Forwarding Methods

This next step is only necessary if you plan to use remote transfer features, such as allowing an extension to transfer to your cell phone or another remote telephone number. You may need to select a call forwarding method.

There are three Call Forwarding Options that the VoicePro can use to transfer callers to another phone number...

WORST: The default is to use two lines to transfer a call. If you want to use this method, then you can skip this step. But it is the worst way to accomplish a transfer because it will tie up two lines while a caller is connected to the destination phone number.

BETTER: An alternative is to use three-way-calling. But this will only work if you have three-way-calling service from your local phone company on all the lines that are connected to the VoicePro. This method will make a transfer using only one line, and it will hold onto the call with the two parties until either party hangs up, or until 120 seconds elapse (with a warning prompt). To keep the conversation going, press # or to extend the call another 120 seconds or press * to extend the call indefinitely and eliminate any further prompts.

BEST: An even better alternative is to transfer the caller and then hang up to free up the line. Freeing up the line allows the VoicePro to accept additional calls while the two parties are talking. This will only work if you subscribe to a "Transfer and Disconnect" type of three-way-calling. This is known as Centrex in some locations. Check with your local phone company.

Select the Forwarding Method

If you plan to use call forwarding for any reason, you need to specify the proper method to be used.

1. Enter Programming Mode.

2. Enter Program Function 37# (Call Forwarding Method).

3. When prompted, enter 0# to have all calls forwarded on two lines with supervision. This is the default.

4. Or press 1# to use the three-way-calling method.

5. Or press 2# to use Transfer and Disconnect if you have Centrex lines.

6. Or press 3# to use two lines but with blind transfer mode.

7. Press * * to end programming and hang up.

Info/Announcement Greetings

There are 99 greetings that you can use for recording informational announcements, menu prompts, or assign as company greetings for day, night and weekend time periods.

All greetings play the main greeting **0** (see next page) unless they are individually recorded differently.

Use Program Function 25 to record the greetings (1-99). You can then assign each greeting to specific lines and if it should be used for day (Program Function 22), night (Program Function 23) or weekend (Program Function 24) greetings when answering a call. You can also assign greetings to menu keys to create Voice-On-Demand announcements (Program Function 44).

The Main Greeting

The Main Greeting is greeting **0** that can be changed with Program Function 21. There are 99 additional greetings (1 thru 99) that can be created with Program Function 25. They all play the Main Greeting **0** until they are individually changed. The default for greeting **0** is...

> "Thank you for calling. If you know your party's number, please enter it now. Otherwise for a directory, press 9. Or for an operator, press zero."

 **Important Tip:** If you plan to use different greetings for day, night and weekend, or if you need to play different greetings on each phone line, then use Function 25 to record all the greetings you need. In this case do not use greeting **0**. Instead, use greetings 1 thru 99 and assign them as needed. Program Functions 22, 23 and 24 are used to assign greetings to the day, night and weekend, respectively. These functions also let you assign various greetings to different lines.

Let's start by using the default greeting until you get everything going. You can decide how you want the VoicePro to answer the phone later. An example you may like to consider is...

> "Thank you for calling. If you know your party's extension you may enter it at any time. Or for immediate assistance, press 0."

Automated Attendant Preparation

The Auto Attendant is a menu system that allows the caller to select the desired option to route their call or to listen to further information. Calls can be routed to an extension or to a mailbox. If transferred to an extension, that station's phone will ring while the caller hears music on hold (if you connected a music source to the VoicePro). If there is no answer, the caller will be routed to the extension's mailbox. With a direct transfer to a mailbox, or after an extension does not answer, the caller will hear the personal greeting of that mailbox and then they may leave a message.

The Auto Attendant can also play other information to the caller. This is done by recording messages in greetings (1 thru 99) with function 25 and then assigning the greetings to various menu option keys with function 44. You also need to record the appropriate prompts in the main company greeting to guide your caller.

The Auto Attendant does not have to answer the call immediately. You may choose to have the calls ring to extension(s) prior to the Auto Attendant answering the call (See function 30).

If you want your calls answered immediately by the Auto Attendant, and not let any extensions ring unless your caller selects an option that rings to an extension, then you need to change the number of rings for the Auto Attendant to zero so that it answers immediately. Follow these steps...

1. Enter Programming Mode.
2. Enter Program Function 30# (Rings for Auto Attendant).
3. When prompted for the line number, enter 1# for line 1.
4. When prompted for the number of rings, enter 0#.
5. Repeat steps 2 thru 4 for each line.
6. Press * * to end programming and hang up.

You also need to make sure you have the Auto Attendant enabled. This is the default setting, so unless you disabled it, you do not need to bother. Program Function 27 is used to enable/disable the Auto Attendant...

1. Enter Programming Mode.
2. Enter Program Function 27# (Enable/Disable Auto Attendant).
3. When prompted, press 1# to enable the Auto Attendant.
4. Press * * to end programming and hang up.

Above, we just set the Auto Attendant to answer immediately. But if you want to set special ringing assignments so that incoming calls ring to selective extensions *before* the Auto Attendant answers, then two things need to be changed. Use Program Function 30 to specify how many rings should occur before the Auto Attendant answers, and use Program Function 4 to set the ringing assignment for each CO line. By default, line 1 rings to extension 10, line 2 to extension 11... and so on. But you can change that with function 4.

Another thing about the Auto Attendant...If the caller does not dial an extension or mailbox number, the call will be transferred to the operator at station 10. You can disable this and have the system just hang up on the caller if they do not press any keys. This may be necessary if you discover you get a lot of hang up calls to the operator. Disable this as follows...

1. Enter Programming Mode.
2. Enter Program Function 39#.
3. When prompted, press 2# to disconnect on no response.
4. Press * * to end programming and hang up.

Set up the Operator Mailbox

The next step is setting up the operator mailbox (10). You need at least this mailbox although there are 99 mailboxes you can assign. Mailboxes 10 and up belong to their matching extensions. The rest are for any voice mail use. When a caller presses option 0 they are transferred to extension 10. This is the operator extension. If there is no answer then the system will play the greeting in mailbox 10 and take a message into this mailbox.

Note: Extension 10 is the operator station and cannot be changed. Callers that dial 0 while in Auto Attendant mode will automatically be transferred to the operator station at extension 10.

To log into mailbox 10, pick up extension 10 and dial *300. The system will ask for the password for mailbox 10. (Dialing *300 works on any extension to log into that extension's mailbox). If you want to log into mailbox 10 from another extension, then dial *310 and then another *. The system will ask for the mailbox password.

Once you log in to the mailbox, press 9 to program this voice mailbox and you will hear the following prompts...

"To change password, press 1.
To record your greeting, press 2.
To program message alert, press 3.
Or to return to the previous menu, press zero."

Go ahead and press 2 and follow the prompts to record your mailbox greeting. The operator extension is now ready for use and you have completed the necessary setup to begin using your VoicePro.

If you want to have custom menus for your Auto Attendant, we'll walk-you-through the programming process in the following section.

Auto Attendant Programming

If you completed the programming in the previous sections, you are now ready to start using your VoicePro. Give it a try. Call you main number and the Auto Attendant will answer with the main greeting you recorded with Program Function 21. It will then wait for you to enter a 2-digit extension or a 1-digit option from the menu.

Now, in this section, we get to the good part: Customizing your menus. Here we will program various menu options based on your needs. This is where the power of your VoicePro will start to become obvious. Just follow along with the segment(s) below that best fit your needs for a walk-through of the programming process.

Single Auto Attendant For All Lines

You need to record a single company greeting.

1. Enter Programming Mode.
2. Enter Program Function 21# (Record main greeting).
3. Record your company welcome greeting, including prompts for which keys to press.
4. Press * * to end programming and hang up.

There's no need to assign this greeting to any lines because greeting 0 is already assigned to all lines for day, night and weekend.

Auto Attendant with Different Greeting per Line

This discussion assumes two lines with a different greeting for each. You need to record the two greetings and then assign them to the lines.

1. Enter Programming Mode.

2. Enter Program Function 25# (Record system greetings).

3. Enter greeting number 1, followed by the # key.

4. Record the welcome greeting for line 1.

5. Enter Program Function 25# (Record system greetings).

6. Enter greeting number 2 followed by the # key.

7. Record the welcome greeting for line 2.

8. Enter Program Function 22# (Assign Greetings to Lines for Day Mode)

9. When prompted to enter the greeting number, enter 1#.

10. When prompted to enter the line number, enter 1#.

11. Enter Program Function 22# (Assign Greetings to Lines for Day Mode)

12. When prompted to enter the greeting number, enter 2#.

13. When prompted to enter the line number, enter 2#.

14. Press * * to end programming and hang up.

Auto Attendant with Day/Night/Weekend Mode

This discussion assumes four incoming lines are being used. You need to record the three greetings and then assign them to all lines for each mode.

1. Enter Programming Mode.
2. Enter Program Function 25# (Record system greetings).
3. Enter greeting number 1 followed by the # key.
4. Record the welcome greeting for day mode.
5. Enter Program Function 25# (Record system greetings).
6. Enter greeting number 2 followed by the # key.
7. Record the welcome greeting for night mode.
8. Enter Program Function 25# (Record system greetings).
9. Enter greeting number 3 followed by the # key.
10. Record the welcome greeting for weekend mode.
11. Enter Program Function 22# (Assign Greetings to Lines for Day Mode)
12. When prompted to enter the greeting number, enter 1#.
13. When prompted to enter the line number(s), enter 1234#.
14. Enter Program Function 23# (Assign Greetings to Lines for Night Mode)
15. When prompted to enter the greeting number, enter 2#.
16. When prompted to enter the line number(s), enter 1234#.
17. Enter Program Function 24# (Assign Greetings to Lines for Weekend Mode)
18. When prompted to enter the greeting number, enter 3#.
19. When prompted to enter the line number(s), enter 1234#.
20. Press * * to end programming and hang up.

Auto Attendant Menu with Voice-On-Demand

Let's say you want to create a menu with three options. Each plays some information to your caller. Plan what you will record for these three items. You will record all three of these under three separate greetings. You will also need to assign these greetings to three menu option keys. And don't forget that you also need to record a main greeting with prompts for the three items.

Let's call the three information greetings Product Info, Prices, and Travel Directions. Now the important thing to understand is that after each recording, you need to also include the prompts for the three items again. This is because the system will wait for user input after playing any greeting. And your caller can select any of the other options or the same again. Let's get started. We'll use greetings 11, 12 and 13 although you could use simply 1, 2 and 3 if you didn't already use these for something else. These greetings need to be assigned to the respective menu options. The main greeting is always greeting **0** unless you want to assign another greeting to a line.

1. Enter Programming Mode.

2. Enter Program Function 21 (Record main greeting).

3. Record your main company greeting, including prompts for which keys to press.

   Example:

   > "Thank you for calling.
   > If you know the extension you wish to reach you may enter it at any time.
   > Or for product information, press 1.
   > For our prices, press 2.
   > For directions to our office, press 3."

4. Enter Program Function 25# (Record system greetings).

5. Enter greeting number 11 followed by the # key.

6. Record your product info.

7. Enter Program Function 25# (Record system greetings).

8. Enter greeting number 12 followed by the # key.

9. Record your pricing info.

10. Enter Program Function 25# (Record system greetings).

11. Enter greeting number 13 followed by the # key.

12. Record your travel directions.

13. Enter Program Function 44# (Assign Menu Keys).

14. When prompted to enter the menu option number, enter 1#.

15. When prompted for assignment type, enter 3# to indicate a greeting.

16. When prompted for the greeting number, enter 11#

17. Enter Program Function 44# (Assign Menu Keys).

18. When prompted to enter the menu option number, enter 2#.

19. When prompted for assignment type, enter 3# to indicate greeting.

20. When prompted for the greeting number, enter 12#.

21. Enter Program Function 44# (Assign Menu Keys).

22. When prompted to enter the menu option number, enter 3#.

23. When prompted for assignment type, enter 3# to indicate greeting.

24. When prompted for the greeting number, enter 13#.

25. Press * * to end programming and hang up.

Auto Attendant Menu with Transfer Options

Your callers can dial any existing extension, or they can select menu key options for various people of departments. Either way, if there is no answer or the extension is busy then the caller will hear the greeting in the matching mailbox and will be able to leave a message. Let's say you have extension 11 in your sales department and extension 12 is your Tech Support. Let's build a menu for this by assigning these extensions to the respective menu options...

1. Enter Programming Mode.

2. Enter Program Function 21 (Record main greeting).

3. Record your main company greeting, including prompts for which keys to press. Example:

   > "Thank you for calling.
   > If you know the extension you wish to reach you may enter it at any time.
   > Or for sales, press 1.
   > For tech support, press 2."

4. Enter Program Function 44# (Assign Menu Keys).

5. When prompted to enter the menu option number, enter 1# for your sales menu option in the example above.

6. When prompted for the type of assignment, enter 2# to indicate an extension.

7. When prompted for the extension number, enter 11#

8. Enter Program Function 44# (Assign Menu Keys).

9. When prompted to enter the menu option number, enter 2# for Tech Support.

10. When prompted for the type of assignment, enter 2# to indicate an extension.

11. When prompted for the extension number, enter 12#

12. Press * * to end programming and hang up.

Auto Attendant Menu with Mailbox Options

There may be reason why you will want menu options that go directly to a mailbox rather than transfer to an extension. Say you want to offer your caller the option listen to information about your products and follow it with an option to let the caller leave their name and address for a brochure to be mailed. Choose a mailbox, say mailbox 50, and assign as follows to menu option 5...

1. Enter Programming Mode.

2. Enter Program Function 21 (Record main greeting).

3. Record your main company greeting, including prompts for which keys to press.

   Example:

   > "Thank you for calling.
   > If you know the extension you wish to reach you may enter it at any time.
   > For information about our products, press 5."

1. Enter Program Function 44# (Assign Menu Keys).

2. When prompted to enter the menu option number, enter 5#.

3. When prompted for the type of assignment, enter 1# to indicate a mailbox.

4. When prompted for the mailbox number, enter 50#

5. Press * * to end programming and hang up.

Programming Multi-Layered Menus

Menus are single level. Menu options go from 1 thru 99 and are actually global. That is, they are not isolated to any specific menu. So if you want to have multiple menus, you need use unique menu options numbers. In other words, if you use menu options 1 and 2 in the main menu, you need to use other options in lower menus. That is the nature of the VoicePro. But you can use 2-digit option numbers all the way up to 99. For example, use 11 thru 19 in one menu and 21 thru 29 in the next menu. And so on.

This is best shown with an example. Record the main greeting...

"For product descriptions, press 1.
For sales, press 2."

1. Record greeting number 1 with the product menu below.
2. Assign greeting 1 to menu option 1.
3. Assign menu option 2 to your sales department extension.

Here is the product menu you might have recorded in greeting 1...

"For our yellow widgets, press 21.
For our blue widgets, press 22."

Now, if you are with me, you can see how you can create a multi-level menu structure even though all menu options exists no matter what level the caller is in with the menu sequence.

Programming Your Extensions

The VP206 has extensions 10 thru 15 and the VP412 goes up to extension 21.

When you pick up any extension phone, you will hear an outside dialtone and you can dial as normal. To dial from one extension to another, press * for an inside dialtone, then the two-digit extension.

You should have the main phone connected to extension 10. This is the operator extension. It will ring when a caller presses "0", although you can reprogram "0" to do anything else, as explained later.

Outside callers can dial any two-digit extension when they hear your company greeting. You can also assign menu options to ring to any extension or even to a group if extensions simultaneously.

Tip: To dial direct into a mailbox rather than a live extension, dial 3 plus the extension number (Such as 315 for extension 15).

Note: Never connect two phones to a single extension jack. If you want to ring multiple phones, you can program the unit to do that with Function 44 as explained on page 92.

Door Phone Intercom Box

A separate door chime intercom box can be installed so that you can communicate, through a station extension, with a guest ringing your doorbell. See page 104 for programming and usage.

Mailbox Numbering

The mailboxes share the same numbering plan as the extensions. Whenever you are prompted for a mailbox number of a user, simply enter their two-digit mailbox number (12 instead of 312). You only need to dial a 3 in front of the mailbox number if you want to dial into a mailbox when the system is expecting you to dial an extension.

Dialing Restriction

Extensions may be set to follow toll-restriction and toll-allow tables on a per extension setting. Toll restriction may be set to disallow long distance calls. You may restrict any number or combination of numbers from being dialed. You may also program exceptions to the restrictions.

Example: Restrict 1 from being dialed as the first digit of an outside call, but you may choose to allow 1-800, 1-888, 1-877 and 1-866.

Use Program Functions 42 and 43 to specify these restrictions for extensions.

Group Ringing

You can program multiple extensions to ring when a one or two digit number is dialed on an Auto Attendant menu. This is known as departmental or group dialing and is normally only found on larger PBX systems. Use Program Function 44 to assign Menu keys to extensions. When prompted for the extension, just include all the extensions in the group before pressing the # key to complete the entry.

Recording Your Voice Mail Greeting

To log into your own voicemail, dial *300. The system will ask for the password for your mailbox. Enter your password followed by #.

To log into a different mailbox from another extension, dial *3xx (where xx is the other mailbox number). In this case you will hear the greeting to know you dialed the right mailbox. Press * during or after the greeting and the system will ask for the password. Enter the password of THAT mailbox followed by #.

After logging in, you will hear your main voice mail menu...

You have one new message and two saved messages. To play the first message, press 1. To undelete all previously deleted messages, press 7. To program your voice mailbox, press 9.

Press 9 and you will hear your maintenance menu options...

To change your password, press 1. To record your greeting, press 2. To setup message alert, press 3.

Complete details on using voicemail is in the section "How to Access Your Mailbox" starting on page 114.

Save Space of Unused Extensions

By default, mailboxes 10 thru 15 on the VP206 and 10 thru 21 on the VP412 play a greeting and take a message.

To avoid filling up memory space of unused mailboxes, you can prevent mailboxes from taking messages by changing the password to something that starts with a "*" (this sets the mailbox to greeting-only). Function 26 (change password) will not change the status of a mailbox, so you have to log into each individually.

Auto Attendant Menu with Pseudo Extensions

You can program additional extensions that are not physical phones to give an impression of a big office. These will be just voicemail extensions that play a greeting and take a message. As an example, here is how you would create a Pseudo Extension 30 assigned to mailbox 30.

1. Enter Programming Mode.
2. Enter Program Function 44# (Assign Menu Keys).
3. When prompted to enter the menu option number, enter 30#.
4. When prompted for the type of assignment, enter 1# to indicate a mailbox.
5. When prompted for the mailbox number, enter 30#
6. Press * * to end programming and hang up.

If you're thinking, why don't I just tell people to dial 330? You are on the ball, good for you. Yes, you can simply dial 330 from the Auto Attendant and you will get into mailbox 30 and hear its greeting. So if you want to make it look like you have three-digit extensions, you can do this. But remember that all your "real" extensions will only have two digits. So when you are in an internal system menu that requests you to enter an extension, it is just the two-digit extension number you will want to enter.

Extensions with Remote Forwarding

You can forward any extension to another extension, to any mailbox, or to a remote telephone number. This can be done from programming mode with Program Function 16. Or it can be done directly in the extension by dialing * then # and you can skip steps 1 thru 3 below. Programming mode lets you do it from anywhere. Here is how to do it from programming mode...

1. Enter Programming Mode.

2. Enter Program Function 16# (Assign Call Forwarding).

3. When prompted, enter the extension to be forwarded. Then press #.

4. When prompted, enter the number to forward call to (See example below). Then press #.

5. When prompted, press 1 to forward all calls or 2 to forward ring-no-answer only. Then press #.

6. Press * * to end programming and hang up.

Example: Dial 17# to forward calls to extension 17. Dial 317# to forward calls to mailbox 17. Dial an outside phone number (up to 11 digits) to forward calls to a remote number.

Pager Alert

You can set Voice Mail Pager Alert for any extension by logging into the extension's mailbox. For extension 12, log into mailbox 12 by dialing *312. Then press * again to log in...the system will ask you for your mailbox password. Enter it followed by the # key. Once you are logged in, press 9 to program your voice mailbox. You will hear...

> "To change password, press 1.
> To record your greetings, press 2.
> To program message alert, press 3.
> Or to return to the previous menu, press zero."

Select 3 from the above options. Then...

- Press 1 to enable telephone message alert.
- Press 2 to enable pager alert.
- Press 3 to disable message alert.
- Press 4 to set alert number.
- Press 5 to listen to your message alert settings.

From that menu, to enable the pager and specify a pager number, press 2. Or to enter a new pager number, press 4. If you want to disable the pager, press 3.

When entering the pager number to be dialed, enter the pager access number, then [*], then the sequence to be sent to the pager. The [*] key causes a delay to wait for the pager service to answer. You may use multiple [*] entries to add more delay if necessary.

Note: Many pagers require a # key to terminate the sequence to be sent to the pager. You may use this here if needed. For this reason, the VoicePro will not terminate when you press the #, but will instead include it in the program sequence. When you are finished entering the pager number and sequence, wait for the VoicePro to indicate success.

Live Message Alert

Notification of new messages is not limited to pager notification. Notification with VoicePrompts can be received at your cellular phone or any remote telephone. It will allow you to listen to new messages without having to call back.

You can have the VoicePro call you at any remote location and deliver your voice mail messages to you. This is known as Live Message Alert. Log into your mailbox. Once you are logged in, press 9 to program your voice mailbox. You will hear...

> To change password, press 1.
> To record your greetings, press 2.
> To program message alert, press 3.
> Or to return to the previous menu, press zero.

Select 3 from the above options. Then...

- Press 1 to enable telephone message alert.
- Press 2 to enable pager alert.
- Press 3 to disable message alert.
- Press 4 to set alert number.
- Press 5 to listen to your message alert settings.

Select 1 from the above options. When prompted, enter the phone number to be called and wait for the system to confirm. Do not press # unless this is required in the dialing sequence. If you need to change this number later, use option 4 from the above options.

Name Directory

When a caller presses option 9 in the Auto Attendant, they will hear the recording of greeting number 9.

The VoicePro comes preset with greeting 9 saying "The directory is not available." This will be replaced by your recording once you change it. Use Program Function 25 to record your own directory in greeting number 9. When prompted, record the directory by stating the name of each person and their extension and/or mailbox.

> **Example:** "For John Smith, dial 11. For Larry Land, dial 12…etc."

Tip: In your main greeting, tell your caller to press 9 for the company directory.

Extension Station Programming

There are three things you can specify for each station extension. Call forwarding, remote call screening, and extension call screening. This is done via Station Programming.

To enter Station Programming, pick up the extension you want to setup and dial * then #. You will hear…

> "Welcome to station programming.
> For call forwarding setup, press 1 plus #.
> For remote call screening setup, press 2 plus #.
> For extension call screening setup, press 3 plus #."

Call Forwarding Programming

You can reroute calls to your extension via Station Programming or via Program Mode (See Program Function 16).

Enter Station Programming and press 1 to specify where calls to your extension should go. You can also disable forwarding under this option. You can specify another extension, any mailbox, or a remote telephone number. And you can specify forwarding for "all calls" or just "ring-no-answer or busy." Just follow the prompts...

1. When prompted, enter the number to forward call to (See example below). Then press #.

2. When prompted, press 1 to forward all calls or 2 to forward ring-no-answer only. Then press #.

Example: Enter 17# to forward calls to extension 17. Enter 317# to forward calls to mailbox 17. Enter an outside phone number (up to 11 digits) to forward calls to that remote number.

Call Screening Programming

You can enable or disable call screening for calls to your extension or for call transfers to a remote number. This is done via Station Programming as shown on page 58. Only outside callers will be screened. See "Call Screening" on page 106 for full details.

Enter Station Programming and press 2 to set screening for calls transferred to you remote number. Press 3 to set screening for calls to your extension.

The system asks for their name and a brief message, and plays this to you when you answer. You can accept the call or send the caller to voice mail.

Tip: You can change the prompt that asks for the caller's name by using Program Function 32.

Greeting-only Mailboxes

Mailboxes that are not associated with physical extensions default as greeting-only mailboxes. Also known as broadcast-only mailboxes.

Example: The VP412 has mailboxes 10 thru 21 associated with the 12 physical extensions. So mailboxes 10 thru 21 are preset as full-featured mailboxes while mailboxes 1 thru 9 and 22 thru 99 are preset as greeting-only.

VoicePro Model	Physical Extensions	VoiceMail Only
VP206	10 thru 15	1 thru 9 and 16 thru 99
VP412	10 thru 21	1 thru 9 and 22 thru 99

Note: The key element that makes a mailbox a greeting-only mailbox is the type of password used. Numeric passwords make the mailbox a full-featured voice mailbox. Passwords that start with a * will make the mailbox only play a greeting and not take messages.

Note: The password for any mailbox must be 4 to 6 digits long (including the * if it's a greeting-only mailbox).

Note: After a caller listens to the greeting in a greeting-only mailbox they will be given the option to dial another mailbox or return to the main menu.

Note: Greeting-only mailboxes do not take messages. To change one of these mailboxes to a full-featured voice mailbox then change the password to one that starts with a number instead of a *.

Default: Default passwords for Greeting-only mailboxes is **99.

Guide to Programming Functions

Now that we have walked you through some programming, you may want to do your own customization. Programming is done by touch-tone from any extension or remote telephone.

Individual extensions can be programmed, via Station Programming, for the purpose of recording personal mailbox greetings, setting call forwarding, changing personal passwords, or anything related to extensions.

In order to program the system setup and Auto Attendant applications, you need to be in Program Mode to use the following Program Functions. Only System Administrators who know the System Password can access Programming Mode.

The following few pages contain a handy "Quick Reference Program Function Table." Note that there are some functions marked *Unused.* This is due to programming changes from older versions. The unused functions have been replaced with enhanced functions under different Function Numbers. Detailed explanations of each Program Function follow the table.

Useful Tip: The ^{M} symbol next to Function Numbers means that Program Function may be monitored with Program Function 50. This enables you to check a program's settings before making any actual changes to the settings.

Quick Reference Program Function Table

Program Function Number	Program Name	Default Setting / Comments
1	System Password	1234#
2 M	Telephone Lines Installed	1 2 3 4
3 M	Telephone Line Access	All Lines. All Extensions
4 M	Telephone Ringing Assignment	Line 1 to Extension 10 Line 2 to Extension 11 etc.
5 M	Door Ring Assignment	None
6 M	Door Port Assignment	None
7 M	Fax Extension	(See also Program Function 31)
8 M	Hold Recall Time-out	180 Seconds
9 M	Prime Line Select	Extension 10: Line 1 Extension 11: Line 2 etc.
10 M	Voice Message Length	120 Seconds
11 M	Greeting Length	120 Seconds
12 M	Night Mode Time Set	3:00AM to 3:01AM (See Function 33 for Weekend Time Set)
13	*(Unused)*	
14 M	Ring-No-Answer Time-out	Default: 6 Rings Ring Forever: set to 0

Program Function Number	Program Name	Default Setting / Comments
15	*(Unused)*	
16 ᴹ	Call Forwarding Assignment	None
17 ᴹ	Remote Call Screening	None
18 ᴹ	Extension Call Screening	None
19	Time Set	12:01AM
20	Date Set	January 1
21 ᴹ	Record Main Greeting 0	Assigned to all lines for Day, Night, & Weekend. (See also Function 25)
22 ᴹ	Day Greeting Line Assignment	Default is Greeting 0 on all lines.
23 ᴹ	Night Greeting Line Assignment	Default is Greeting 0 on all lines.
24 ᴹ	Weekend Greeting Line Assignment	Default is Greeting 0 on all lines.
25 ᴹ	Record Greetings: You may record up to 99 greetings and assign them to Menu Options (Function 44) or to Lines for Day, Night, Weekend (Functions 22, 23, 24).	Default Greeting: "Thank you for calling. If you know your party's number, please enter it now. Otherwise, for a directory press 9. Or for an operator, press zero."
26	Reset Mailbox Password	4321 for Regular mailboxes. **99 for greeting-only boxes.
27 ᴹ	Enable/Disable Automated Attendant	Enabled

Program Function Number	Program Name	Default Setting / Comments
28	*(Unused)*	
29 M	Message Waiting Light	All enabled. If disabled, stutter dialtone is used instead.
30 M	Rings Before Auto Attendant Answers	3 for each line
31 M	Fax CO Line(s)	None (See also Prog. Function 7)
32 M	Record Call Screening Greeting	Default: "Please record your name and a short message at the tone."
33 M	Weekend Mode Time Set	Sun 3:00AM to Sun 3:01AM. (See Function 12 for Night Time Set)
34	*(Unused)*	
35	All Mailbox Message Check	Single step to hear which mailboxes have messages.
36	*(Unused)*	
37 M	Call Forwarding Method	(0 below is the default) 0: 2-line conference, supervised. 1: Three-way calling. 2: Centrex (frees up line). 3: Two-line conference, blind transfer.
38	*(Unused)*	
39 M	Rotary Dial Support (No Touch Tone)	If no response: Disconnect or Go to Operator (default)
40 M	CO Hook Flash Time	0.5 seconds (500 ms)
41 M	Volume Adjustment	System: 23 Greetings: 21

Program Function Number	Program Name	Default Setting / Comments
42 ᴹ	Toll Restrict Station Extensions	None
43 ᴹ	Toll Restrictions and Exceptions	None
44 ᴹ	Assign Menu Keys: Any keys from 1 to 99, other than valid extensions, may be assigned to an extension (10-21), to a mailbox (10-99), or to play a greeting (0-99)	Defaults: 0 is Operator (Extension10). 1 thru 8 is not assigned. 9 is the Name Directory (it plays greeting number 9).
50	Monitor System Settings	Review settings for Program Functions marked ᴹ
91	Hardware Version	Speaks installed hardware version.
92	Software Version	Speaks installed software version.
93	Message Memory Space Available	See page 94 for details.
99	System Reset	Default System
* *	Exit Programming	

Note Function 50 in the table above. You will find this to be a very useful function and you will want to use it often. This function is used to monitor the present setting of most other Program Functions without making any actual changes to them. All Program Functions listed above with an ᴹ can be monitored.

Detailed explanation of all the above Program Functions begins on the following page.

Program Functions Explained

You need to be in Program Mode to use the following Program Functions. Only System Administrators who know the System Password can access Programming Mode.

While in programming mode, if you do not make an entry within one minute after the prompt, the system will hang up and terminate the session. Valid entries made to that point are retained in the system.

If you exited programming mode from the previous section, you must return to program mode; otherwise, proceed to select from the programs outlined below.

Useful Tip: The ᴹ symbol means this program may be monitored without changing the programmed settings by using Program Function 50.

Program Function 1:
System Password

1) In programming mode, enter 1#.

2) When prompted for a new password, enter a 4-digit password, then #.

3) When asked to re-enter password, enter it again and then press #.

Default: 1234.

Important: Remember your password. If you forget your password, you must either use the hardware-reset button, which returns system program settings to their default states.

Program Function 2:
Telephone Lines Installed ᴹ

1) In programming mode, press 2#.

2) Enter the line numbers actually connected to the CO lines.

- If one line is installed, press 1.
- If two lines are installed, enter 1 2.
- If three lines are installed, enter 1 2 3.
- If four lines are installed, enter 1 2 3 4.

3) Press #.

Default: 1,2 for the VP206 and 1,2,3,4, for the VP412

Program Function 3:
Telephone Line Access ᴹ

This program determines which extensions may access which telephone lines.

1) In programming mode, enter 3#.

2) When prompted for a line number, press 1 (for Line 1), and then press #.

3) When prompted for the extension number, enter *all* extension numbers in succession and then press #. For example, if extensions 10 and 11 are to be assigned, then press 1011#.

4) Repeat for lines 2 through 4.

Default: All incoming telephone lines are accessible from all connected extension stations.

Program Function 4:
Telephone Ringing Assignment ᴹ

This program determines the extensions to ring for each incoming line. The Auto Attendant will override this program when it is set to 0 rings (Program Function 30). Also the Fax line assignment (Program Function 31) will override this program if activated.

1) In programming mode, enter 4#.

2) When prompted for a line number, press 1 (for Line 1), and then press #.

3) When prompted for the extension number, enter *all* extension numbers in succession and then press #. For example, if extensions 10 and 11 are to be assigned, then press 1011#.

4) Repeat steps 1 thru 3 for additional lines.

Default: Line 1 rings on station 10, Line 2 on station 11, Line 3 on station 12 and line 4 on station 13.

Program Function 5:
Door Phone Ring Assignment ᴹ

If you are using a door phone intercom, use Function 6 (see next page) to assign the extension you connect it to. And use this function to specify the extension(s) to ring when a visitor at the door presses the intercom button.

1) In programming mode, enter 5#

2) When prompted for the extension number, enter *all* extension numbers in succession that the door intercom is to ring on, and then press #. For example, if extensions 10 and 11 are to be assigned, then press 1011#.

Additional Programming: See also Program Function 6.

Program Function 6:
Door Phone Port Assignment ^M

If you are using a door phone intercom, use this function to assigned the extension to which it is attached. You can use any phone as an the intercom. When you pick up the receiver, the VoicePro will immediately ring all extensions specified with Function 5 (see last page).

1) In programming mode, enter 6#.

2) When prompted for an extension number, enter the extension port where the door phone is connected, and then press #.

3) To disable ringing extensions, just press # in step 2 above.

Default: None

Additional Programming: See also Program Function 5.

Program Function 7:
Fax Station Line Assignment ^M

All incoming fax calls on the specified CO lines will be switched to the assigned fax extension automatically. This is the extension where you will connect your fax machine.

1) In programming mode, enter 7#.

2) When prompted for the fax station line assignment, enter the extension where you have your fax machine, then #.

Default: None

Additional Programming: You also need to specify which CO lines should detect fax. Do this with Program Function 31.

Program Function 8:
Hold Recall Time-out ᴹ

Calls placed on hold, or in a park orbit, will ring back, on timeout, to the station that initiated the hold. If the extension that receives the ring back does not answer, the caller on hold will be transferred to that extension's mailbox to leave a voicemail message.

1) In programming mode, enter 8#.
2) When prompted to set the timer, enter the number, in seconds, followed by #. For example, if you want the station to ring back in 30 seconds, enter 30#.

Default: 180 seconds.

Program Function 9:
Prime Line Selection ᴹ

A prime line is the CO line that an extension will select first for outside dialing. This means it will provide dial tone from this line when one picks up that extension. If that line is in use, it will provide dialtone from the next available line in sequence, searching from line 1 if no higher lines are available.

In programming mode, enter 9#.

1) When prompted for the extension number, then press #.
2) Next, when prompted, enter the prime CO line to be used for this extension. For line 1, press 1#, for line 2, press 2#, etc. Repeat function 9 for each extension.

Default: Extension 10 starts with line 1, 11 starts with line 2, etc.

Note: A stutter dialtone indicates all lines are in use and only inside extensions may be dialed. In this case you do not need to dial * before the extension when dialing since you already have inside dialtone.

Program Function 10:
Voice Mail Message Length ᴹ

Specify the allowable recording time for leaving messages.

1) In programming mode, enter 10#.

2) When prompted to set the voice message length enter the number in seconds and then press #.

Default: 120 seconds.

Tip: If you want to limit a caller's message to one minute then enter 60# (time in seconds).

Note: The maximum allowable length is 9999 seconds. But it is not recommended to allow more than 300 seconds for messages.

Program Function 11:
Greeting Length ᴹ

Specify the allowable maximum recording time for greetings.

1) In programming mode, enter 11#.

2) When prompted to set the greeting length enter the number in seconds and then press #.

Default: 120 seconds.

Tip: If you want to record greetings or announcements up to five minutes long then enter 300# (time in seconds).

Note: The maximum allowable greeting length is 9999 seconds.

71

Program Function 12:
Night Mode Time Set ᴹ

During night mode, the Auto Attendant automatically answers all lines and plays the night greeting.

1) In programming mode, enter 12#.
2) Enter the hour (1 – 12)) night mode is to start, then press #.
3) Enter the minute (00 – 59), then press #.
4) Press 1 for AM or 2 for PM, then press #.
5) Enter the hour (1 – 12) night mode is to end, then press #.
6) Enter the minute (00 – 59) and then press #.
7) Press 1 for AM or 2 for PM, and then press #.

Example: If you want to start night mode at 5:00 PM and stop at 9:00 AM, enter 5#00#2#9#00#1#.

Default: The default is 3:00 AM to 3:01 AM.

Important: Night mode cannot be disabled. Instead, set night mode to start and end in one minute when there is minimal telephone traffic, as the default above.

Related programming Note: Use Program Function 23 to assign the night greeting.

Related programming Note: See also Function 33 for setting the time period for Weekend Mode.

Program Function 14:
Ring-No-Answer Time-out ᴹ

This function allows you to set the number of rings that extensions will ring before transferring to the extension's voicemail.

1) In programming mode, enter 14#.

2) When prompted to set the "ring-no-answer timeout" enter the number and then press #.

Default: 6 rings.

Tip: You can completely disable voicemail by setting this value to zero rings. It will ring forever and never go to voice mail.

Program Function 16:
Call Forwarding Assignment ᴹ

You can forward an extension to another extension, to your mailbox, or to a remote telephone number.

1) In programming mode, enter 16#.

2) Enter the extension number to be forwarded and then press #.

3) Enter the number to which to forward calls, then press #.
   Example: Dial 17# to forward calls to extension station 17. Dial 317# to forward calls to mailbox 17. Dial an outside phone number (up to 11 digits) to forward calls remotely.

4) Press 1 for all calls or 2 for Ring-No-Answer. Then press #.

Default: No call forwarding programmed.

Note: Call forwarding uses the forwarding method specified in Program Function 37.

Call Forwarding notes continue on the next page...

▦ **Note:** Call Forwarding can also be enabled or disabled via Station Programming, without entering system programming. See "Call Forwarding" on page 110 for full details.

▦ **Note:** Call forwarding only works when the Auto Attendant is enabled.

▯**Important:** If a call is answered by someone and then transferred to a call forwarded extension, the call will not follow forwarding. It will just ring that extension to which the caller was manually transferred. If no answer, then he or she is forwarded to that extension's mailbox.

Program Function 17:
Remote Call Screening ᴹ

You can use this function, instead of function 16, to specify that you want to screen your forwarded calls. The system will announce the name of the caller and you can accept or reject the call. See "Call Screening" on page 106 for full details.

1) In programming mode, enter 17#.

2) When prompted, enter the station number to be screened and then press #.

3) Next enter the outside number to forward calls to, then #.

Default: No remote screening.

▦ **Note:** This feature can be enabled or disabled via Station Programming without entering system programming.

▯**Important:** Call screening requires two lines and does NOT use the forwarding method specified in Program Function 37.

Program Function 18:
Extension Call Screening ᴹ

You can use this program to specify that you want to screen your calls at your extension when receiving a call. The system will announce the name of the caller and you can accept or reject the call. See "Call Screening" on page 106 for full details.

1) In programming mode, enter 18#.

2) When prompted enter the station number to be screened and then press #.

Default: No local screening.

Note: This feature can be enabled or disabled via station programming without entering system programming.

Program Function 19:
Set System Time

1) In programming mode, enter 19#.

2) Enter the hour (1 – 12) and then press #.

3) Enter minutes (00 – 59) and then press #.

4) Press 1 for AM or 2 for PM and press #.

Example: To set the time to 3:04 PM, dial 3#04#2#.

Default: 12:00 PM

Program Function 20:
Set System Date

Sets the current date: month, day, year and day of the week.

1) In programming mode, enter 20#.

2) Enter the month (1 – 12), then press #.

   For example, press 3 for March or 9 for September.

3) Enter the day (1 thru 31), then press #.

4) Enter the year as two digits, then press #.
   For example, enter 05 for 2005.

5) Enter the day of the week and then press #. Use the numbers from the following table:

   1 = Monday
   2 = Tuesday
   3 = Wednesday
   4 = Thursday
   5 = Friday
   6 = Saturday
   7 = Sunday

Example: To set the date to Sunday, May 15, 2005, dial 5#15#05#7#.

Default: Thursday, January 1, 1998.

Program Function 21:
Record Main Greeting ᴹ

This function is used to record the main greeting (greeting 0). However it is recommended that you do not use greeting 0. Instead, use Program Function 25, which lets you record any of the 99 greetings, which can be assigned for different lines or for day, night and weekend mode. You assign those greetings using Program Functions 22, 23, and 24.

1) In programming mode, enter 21#.

2) When prompted begin recording your new main greeting after the tone.

3) Press # to save your recording.

Default: Greeting 0 is the main greeting for all lines in day, night and weekend mode of operation unless you assign other greetings 1 thru 99 using program functions 22, 23, 24 or 44.

Warning: Once greeting 0 has been recorded the system cannot play the default greeting again. However, should you desire to keep the default greeting for later use, you can record and assign any other greeting from 1 thru 99.

Important Tip: Rather than using Program Function 21 for greeting 0, use Program Function 25 to record greetings 1 thru 99. You can then assign different greetings on a per line basis (Program Function 15), or for day (Program Function 22), night (Program Function 23) or weekend mode (Program Function 24). You can also assign greetings to menu keys (Program Function 44).

Program Function 22:
Daytime Greeting Assignment ᴹ

Use this program if you want to have a different greeting for incoming lines for daytime operation. Individual lines can be programmed with different greetings for daytime mode.

1) In programming mode, enter 22#.

2) When prompted to enter the greeting number, enter the greeting number (1-99) then press #.

3) When prompted to enter the line number, enter the line or lines to play the selected greeting, followed by #.
   Example: Enter 12# for both lines 1 and 2.

Default: Greeting 0 is assigned to all lines for day, night and weekend mode of operation. It is best to use greetings 1 thru 99 to allow for programming flexibility.

📖 **Related programming Note:** Use Program Function 25 to record greetings 1 thru 99. These can be assigned to individual lines, or used as different greetings for day, night and weekend.

📖 **Related programming Note:** Use Program Function 30 to set the number of rings to the assigned telephones before the Auto Attendant answers. Setting rings to **0** will cause the Auto Attendant to answer immediately in day mode of operation. At night it answers immediately anyway.

📖 **Related programming Note:** Use Program Function 4 to assign which extensions will ring before the Auto Attendant answers the call. The number of rings before the Auto Attendant (Program Function 30) only applies to day mode of operation. When the system is in night mode the Auto Attendant answers immediately and plays the specified night greeting assigned with Program Function 23.

Program Function 23:
Nighttime Greeting Assignment ᴹ

Use this program if you want to have a different greeting for incoming lines for nighttime operation. Individual lines can be programmed with different greetings for nighttime mode.

1) In programming mode, enter 23#.

2) When prompted to specify the greeting, enter the greeting number (1-99), then press #. Example: 5 #

3) When prompted to enter the line number, enter the line or lines to play the selected greeting, followed by #. Example: 12# (for both lines 1 and 2).

Default: Greeting 0 is assigned to all lines for day, night and weekend mode of operation.

Additional Programming: You also need to specify the night mode time period. See Program Function 12.

Related programming Note: Night mode of operation overrides day mode. When the system is in night mode the Auto Attendant answers immediately and plays the specified night greeting assigned. Use program 25 to record greetings to be assigned. Greetings may be assigned on a per-line basis, and by time period (day, night or weekend mode).

Program Function 24:
Weekend Greeting Assignment ᴹ

Use this program if you want to have a different greeting for incoming lines for weekend operation. Individual lines can be programmed with different greetings for weekend mode.

1) In programming mode, enter 24#.

2) When prompted to specify the greeting, enter the greeting number (1-99), then press #. Example: 6 #

3) When prompted to enter the line number, enter the line or lines to play the selected greeting, followed by #. Example: 34# (for both lines 3 and 4).

Default: Greeting **0** is assigned to all lines for day, night and weekend mode of operation.

Important: You also need to specify the weekend mode time period. See Program Function 33.

Related programming Note: Weekend mode of operation overrides **both** day and night mode. When the system is in weekend mode the Auto Attendant answers immediately and plays the specified weekend greeting assigned. Use program 25 to record greetings to be assigned. Greetings may be assigned on a per-line basis, and by time period (day, night or weekend mode).

Program Function 25:
Record Greetings ᴹ

This Program Function is used to record all system greetings with the exception of the main greeting (greeting **0**), which can only be recorded using Program Function 21.

1) In programming mode, enter 25#.

2) When prompted, enter the greeting number (1-99), then press #. Example: 1 #

3) Begin recording your new greeting after the tone.

4) When finished recording, press #.

Default: All greetings play the main greeting **0** until recorded differently.

📖 **Note:** Greeting number 9 is the default greeting for the company directory. Use greeting 9 only for this purpose since it will be played when a caller presses menu key 9.

Program Function 26:
Reset Mailbox Password

The System Administrator can use this Function to reset the password for extensions to the system default.

1) In programming mode, enter 26#.

2) When prompted, enter the two-digit mailbox number and then press #.

📖 **Note:** If you previously changed the status of a mailbox, it will remain that way and the default password will be set accordingly. Regular mailboxes are reset to 4321 and Greeting-Only mailboxes are reset to **99.

Program Function 27:
Enable/disable Auto Attendant ᴹ

The Automated Attendant provides a custom menu that you can create. Callers can choose options from the menu to route their calls. The Auto Attendant is enabled by default but you can use this function to disable or later enable it again. If you disable the Auto Attendant, then calls will route direct to extensions as specified using Program Function 4.

1) In programming mode, enter 27#.

2) Press 1# to enable the Auto Attendant or press 2# to disable.

Default: The Auto Attendant is enabled unless you disable it.

📖 **Note:** Use Function 23, 23, 24 and 25 to create and assign recorded menus for the Auto Attendant.

Program Function 29:
Message Waiting Light ᴹ

Telephones must have a 90-volt message light for this feature to operate. Use this Function to enable or disable. When disabled, a stutter dialtone will be used instead to indicate new messages.

1) In programming mode, enter 29#.

2) When prompted, enter *all* the extension numbers that use a message-waiting light, then press #. Example: For stations 10, 11 and 12 to light the message-waiting light press 101112#.

3) To disable on all extensions and use the stutter dialtone, just press # alone when prompted for extensions.

Default: All extensions have message waiting light enabled.

📖 **Note:** Telephone sets must be equipped with a 90-volt message-waiting light for this feature to operate.

Program Function 30:
Rings Before Auto Attendant ᴹ

This controls the number of rings to the extension(s) before the Auto Attendant takes over. If you want the Auto Attendant to answer immediately, enter zero for the number of rings.

1) In programming mode, enter 30#.
2) When prompted, press 1 (for line 1), then press #.
3) Enter the number of rings (0 thru 99), and then press #.
4) Repeat steps 1 thru 3 to program for each CO line.

Default: 3 rings for each line.

▨ **Note:** If an extension is busy, the Auto Attendant will answer the next call for that extension without a delay.

Program Function 31:
Fax CO Line Assignment ᴹ

This enables the Auto Attendant to detect faxes on the specified line. If a fax tone is detected, the call is automatically switched to the extension where you have your fax machine (specified with function 7). Function 31 overrides functions 4, 27 and 30 since the Auto Attendant will answer the call if it's not a fax.

1) In programming mode, enter 31#.
2) When prompted, enter the CO line number that will receive fax transmissions, and then press #.
3) At the prompt, press 1# to enable or press 2# to disable.
4) Repeat steps 1 thru 3 for all lines that might receive fax calls.

▨ **Additional programming:** You must also specify which extension has the fax machine attached with Program Function 7.

Program Function 32:
Record Call Screening Greeting ᴹ

When call screening is enabled for any extension, the system will ask the caller to speak their name so that it can play that to you for screening purposes. You can then decide to accept the call or not. The greeting that is used to ask for the caller's name can be changed with this Program Function.

1) In programming mode, enter 32#.
2) After the tone, record your greeting.
3) When finished recording, press #.

Default: "Please record your name and a short message at the tone."

Program Function 33:
Weekend Mode Time Set ᴹ

During weekend mode, the Auto Attendant automatically answers all lines and plays the weekend greeting. When enabled, this program overrides day and night modes.

1) In programming mode, enter 33#.
2) Specify the start day by entering 1 thru 7 from the following table, then press #.

   1 = Monday   5 = Friday
   2 = Tuesday   6= Saturday
   3 = Wednesday   7= Sunday
   4 = Thursday

3) Enter the start hour (1 thru 12), then press #.
4) Enter the start minute (00 thru 59), then press #.
5) Press 1 for AM or 2 for PM, and then press #.

6) Enter the stop day using the numbers listed in step 2.
7) Enter the stop hour (1 thru 12), then press #.
8) Enter the stop minute (00 thru 59), then press #.
9) Press 1 for AM or 2 for PM, and then press #.

Default: Starts Sunday 3:00 AM and ends Sunday 3:01 AM.

Important: Weekend mode cannot be disabled. Instead, set weekend mode to start and end in one minute when there is minimal telephone traffic (as shown in the default above).

Additional programming: You also need to assign the weekend greeting. See Program Function 24.

Related programming Note: You may also want to specify a night mode. See Function 12 for setting the time period for Night Mode and Function 23 to assign the greeting for the night mode.

Program Function 35:
All Mailbox Message Check

The System Administrator can review which mailboxes have messages without having to log into each one to find out.

1) In programming mode, enter 35#.
2) Listen as the system announces which mailboxes have messages.

Program Function 37:
Call Forwarding Method ᴹ

The VoicePro can use any of three methods to transfer calls, which you set with this Function. You can use three-way-calling, transfer and disconnect, or use two lines.

1) In programming mode, enter 37#.

2) Select one of the following call forwarding methods:

- Enter 0# to have calls forwarded on 2 lines with supervision. Busy or unanswered calls are forwarded to a voice mailbox.

- Enter 1# to enable one line to have 3-way calling feature. **Note:** You must have 3-way calling service for this feature to operate properly. Also, it will be required to press # every 120 seconds to extend the conversation, or * to extend the call indefinitely without further prompts.

- Enter 2# to enable one line with transfer (free up port at end of dial). **Note:** You must have "transfer and disconnect" (Centrex) lines for this feature to operate properly. Toll charges remain in effect until the transferred call is disconnected.

- Enter 3# to enable 2 lines to have blind transfer capabilities. Busy or unanswered calls are not transferred to a voice mailbox, and will ring until disconnected.

Default: 0# (two lines with supervision).

📖 **Note:** See "Call Forwarding Methods" on page 37 for more details.

Program Function 39:
Rotary Dial Telephone Support ᴹ

Calls from a rotary (pulse) telephone, or in some cases from overseas, are unable to dial any touchtone digits to select options in the Auto Attendant menu. The system can only respond to DTMF (Dial Tone Multi Frequency) dialed digits. Better known as touchtone.

This feature allows specifying how to route callers if they do not dial any digits after the greeting. You can specify that the caller should be transferred to the operator (extension 10) or that they should be disconnected.

The reason you may want to choose to disconnect the caller when there is no response is to prevent false ringing to the operator when people hang up without selecting a menu option. This can happen if your telephone company does not provide positive disconnect signal or your telephone lines are part of a buildings PBX system that is slow in sending positive disconnect, thus tying up your telephone lines for a period of time longer than necessary.

1) In programming mode, enter 39#.
2) When prompted press 1# to transfer to the operator or 2# to disconnect if no response.

When option 1 is selected, calls will transfer to the operator if no touchtone is received. If option 2 is selected, calls with no response will just be disconnected.

Default: Rotary dial telephone support is enabled by default. So you may want to disable it if you get a lot of hang-up calls to the operator.

Program Function 40:
Central Office Hook-flash Time ᴹ

If you have Call Waiting service on your phone lines that are attached to your VoicePro, then you need to be able to do a "Flash" on the outside line when you hear a Call Waiting Tone. You can do this by dialing 52 after pressing the Flash Key on your phone.

The timing of the hook-flash that is sent over the outside CO line can be changed to accommodate different countries flash times to better utilize telephone company features. Telephone company features such as three-way calling, call waiting, and call transfer to another telephone number all require issuing a flash on the CO line. The flash time may be adjusted from 100ms to 500ms.

1) In programming mode, enter 40#.

2) When prompted for the hook-flash time, enter a value from 1 to 7, then press #. 1 means 100ms. 7 means 700 ms.

This function will not change the hook-flash needed to access the VoicePro system features, which is the flash sent from your telephone to the VoicePro system. It will only change the hook-flash sent to the CO lines when you dial 52 after a hook-flash.

Default: 5, which means 500ms.

Caution: Do not change this setting unless you know what you are doing. If you must experiment with this in case it's not working, first try increasing in small increments, such as 6 for 600ms. Then if still not working, try 4 for 400ms. Continue one step at a time first higher then lower.

Program Function 41:
Volume Adjustment ᴹ

The volume of voice prompts, greetings and messages may be changed to better suite your preferences. This Program Function can be used to adjust both the volume level of recorded prompts that are part of the VoicePro system, as well as the volume of voicemail messages and recorded greetings.

1) In programming mode, enter 41#.

2) When prompted, press 1# for system prompt volume level or press 2# for recorded messages volume level.

3) Enter the new volume setting (15 thru 31), then press #.

Repeat this program from the beginning if you desire to change the volume level not selected the first time.

Default: The system prompt volume level is 23. The recorded greetings and messages volume level is 21.

📖 **Note:** It is also possible to increase or decrease the volume while listening to a voicemail message from your mailbox by pressing 7 repetitively to decrease the playback volume, or 9 repetitively to increase the playback volume.

Program Function 42:
Toll Restrict Station Extensions ᴹ

This function assigns extensions that are to be restricted from Long Distance toll calls. Restricted extensions will not be allowed to dial any of the numbers specified with Program Function 43. If a toll number is dialed be any restricted extensions, the outside line will be dropped and the extension user will hear an error/busy tone. Toll restricting an extension only affects the extension's ability to call out on the telephone CO line.

1) In programming mode, enter 42#.

2) When prompted, enter the extension(s) to follow toll restriction.

3) Example: 10111415, for extensions 10, 11, 14 and 15

4) Press #

Default: No extensions are assigned to be toll restricted

Related programming: Set toll restriction and exception numbers with Program Function 43.

Program Function 43:
Toll Restrictions and Exceptions ᴹ

Toll restriction numbers are the numbers to be restricted when an assigned extension attempts to dial that particular number or numbers. For example: If '1' is a restricted number, any extension assigned to follow toll restriction (Program Function 42), would not be allowed to connect, and would result in the line being dropped and error/busy tone issued to that extension. The restricted extensions may still dial local numbers and any combination of numbers as long as the first digit is not a '1'. The most common restriction numbers are 1 and 0.

The exceptions programming will be the allowances that over ride the restrictions. For example: If '1' were the restriction number, you may want to allow the exception of 1-800, 1-888, 1-877 and 1-866, which do start with a '1' but are toll free. If 1-800 is entered as the exception then any digits following 1-800-(XXX-XXXX) would not follow as a restriction, thus allowing all 1-800 calls.

1) In programming mode, enter 43#.

2) When prompted, enter the numbers to be restricted, entering a # between each number(s).
    Example: 1 # 0 # 411 #

3) Press another # when finished with list.

4) When prompted, enter the exceptions to the rule, with a # between each. Example: 1800 # 1888 # 1877 # 1866 #.

5) Press another # when finished with list.

Default: No toll restricted or exceptions assigned.

🕮 **Related programming:** Assign Toll Restriction to extensions with Program Function 42. If you restrict 9 from being dialed, be sure to make the exception entry for 911.

Program Function 44:
Assign Menu Key(s) ᴹ

This program allows you to program the action to be performed for keys in your Auto Attendant menu.

Menu Keys can be one or two digits. The Menu Keys 0 thru 99 (with exceptions noted below) can be assigned to carry out one of three actions...

1. Transfer the caller to an extension.

2. Send caller directly to a mailbox to hear a personal greeting and then leave a voicemail message. If the mailbox is a greeting only mailbox return to the main menu greeting after playing,

3. Play another greeting. Either for another menu or to play announcements.

From the Automated Attendant main greeting you may want to have the caller dial 1 for sales and 2 for customer support. Assign the action of pressing 1 and 2 from the above actions.

1) In programming mode, enter 44#.

2) When prompted for the menu number, enter the Menu Key to be programmed followed by #.

3) When prompted, enter 1# for a mailbox, 2# for extension(s), 3# for a greeting, or 0# to delete the previous setting.

4) When prompted, enter the desired mailbox (2 digits), desired greeting number or if assigning extensions enter *all* the extension numbers that you want to ring for this menu option assignment, then press #. **Example:** For extensions 15, 12, and 10 enter 151210#.

5) Repeat steps 1 thru 4 for all Menu Keys you want to assign.

Which Mailbox takes messages when ringing to multiple extensions?

Did you notice in the prior example that we specified the extensions backwards? If a caller selects the assigned menu key they will be placed on hold and extensions 10, 12 and 15 will begin to ring. If any one of the ringing extensions picks up they will be connected to the caller. But if no one picks up the caller will be transferred to the first extension's mailbox. Therefore mailbox 15 gets the voice mail message in this example.

Defaults:

> Menu Key 0 is assigned to extension 10.
>
> Menu Key 9 is assigned to greeting number 9.

Extensions: All valid extension numbers are assigned by default to transfer to their respective extensions. Valid extension numbers are 10 thru 15 on the VP206 and 10 thru 21 on the VP412.

📖 **Note:** The Menu Key assignments are valid from any greeting (1 thru 99). This means that Menu Keys dialed from greeting 1 will have the same functionality as the same Menu Keys dialed from greeting 2 and so forth. So if you want to program multiple menus you need to use unique Menu Key assignments.

Program Function 50:
Monitor System Settings

This Function is used to monitor a Program Function's setting without making any actual changes. All Program Functions listed above with an ^{M} can be monitored. See page 96 for more info.

1) In programming mode, enter 50#.

2) Enter the Program Function number to monitor its settings, then press #.

Program Function 91:
Hardware Version

1) In programming mode, enter 91#.

2) The system will speak your current hardware version.

Program Function 92:
Software Version

1) In programming mode, enter 92#.

2) The system will speak your current software version.

Program Function 93:
Message Memory Space Available

1) In programming mode, enter 93#.

2) The system will speak ten digits such as 0 2 2 1 2 2 n 0 0 0. The 7th digit, represented as "n" in this example, indicates the total hours of speech recording space installed in your unit, as indicated in the table below. The other digits are not pertinent.

Value of "n"	Hours of Storage
1	1 hour
2	2 hours
3	4 hours
4	8 hours

Program Function 99:
System Reset

This Program Function resets programming to its default values. See detailed explanation on the next page.

What gets reset? The system password, system greetings, and all programming will be reset to factory default and will need to be redone.

What remains unchanged? Individual mailbox greetings, voice mail messages, and mailbox passwords will remain intact.

1) In programming mode, enter 99#.
2) At the prompt, press 1# to confirm system reset or press 2# to cancel your request

Program Function * *:
Exit Programming

Enter the * key twice in a row (* *) to exit programming mode. Hanging up while in programming mode will have the same effect. All new settings will stay set either way.

Program Function #:
Repeat Last Function

If you happened to need to repeat the same Program Function immediately after using it, you may speed thing up by just pressing the # key for the next function. The system will repeat the same function you just used.

Confirm Program Settings

When you need to find out what any program function is set to, you can have the system speak this information to you by using Program Function 50 to monitor the system settings.

1) Enter Programming Mode.

2) Enter Program Function 50# (Monitor System Settings).

3) When prompted for desired program number, enter it, followed with the # key.

4) The system will tell you the settings.

5) Press * * to end programming and hang up.

Factory Reset Button

If the unit fails to start up after applying power, you can reboot the system by pressing the Reset Button. For safety, the reset button is behind a small hole located on the rear of the VoicePro unit. The wire of a paper clip works well to press the reset button.

This is considered a "hardware system reset" and it will delete all voice mail messages and greetings. It also resets all program functions to their default states, including the time and date.

The system will redo a memory check...extension 10 will ring to indicate how much memory is available as it did with initial power up.

There is also a "software system reset" which is done with Program Function 99. A "software reset" will also reset programming to its default values. The System Password and system greetings will be set to the default as well. However, a "software reset" will preserve mailbox greetings, voice mail messages, and mailbox passwords.

Using Your VoicePro System

This section provides you with detailed instructions for using all of the basic and advanced Voice Mail and Phone System features on your VoicePro system. You will learn about the following...

- How To Make Calls
- Flash Key
- Answering Call Waiting
- Alternate Call Pickup
- Conference Calls
- Door Chime Box Usage
- Fax Switching
- Placing A Call On Hold
- Hold Recall
- Call Screening
- Transferring Calls

- Paging All Extensions
- Call Forwarding
- Intercom Calls
- Park and Retrieve A Call
- Recording a Conversation
- Accessing Your Mailbox
- Voice Mail Message Options
- Programming Your Mailbox
- Caller Options
- Accessing Phone Co. Features

How To Make Calls

To make an outbound call

1) Lift the receiver.
2) Listen for dial tone.
3) Dial phone number.

 Note: The system automatically connects to an outside line when you pick up the receiver.

To make an outbound call on a specific line

1) Lift the receiver.
2) Press *.
3) Dial 8 and the line number. (Example: 81 for Line 1, 82 for Line 2, 83 for Line 3 and 84 for Line 4.)
4) Listen for dial tone.
5) Dial phone number.

Tip: This feature can be used for diagnosing phone lines.

To make an internal call

1) Lift the receiver.
2) Listen for dial tone.
3) Press * for internal dial tone.
4) Dial number, for example 10 for Station extension 10 or 310 for voice mailbox 10.

To make an internal call while on another call

1) Press Flash to receive an internal dial tone.
2) Dial other number.
3) Press Flash to return to previous call.

Flash Key

The flash key on your telephone activates certain **VoicePro** features such as call transfer, conference calling, and putting a caller on hold.

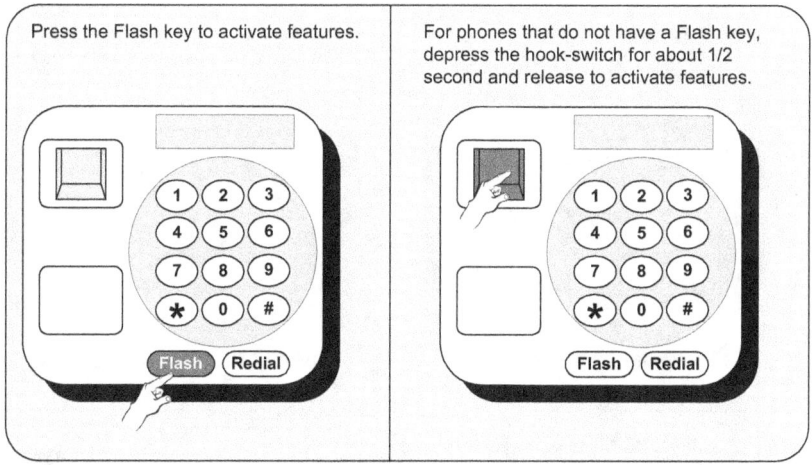

Note: If you do not have a Flash Key on your phone, you can still do a Flash by pressing the "Hook-switch" for half a second.

How To Answer Call Waiting

If you have Call Waiting service on the phone lines attached to your VoicePro, then you need to be able to do a "Flash" on the outside line when you hear a Call Waiting Tone. You can do this by dialing **5 2** after pressing the Flash Key on your phone.

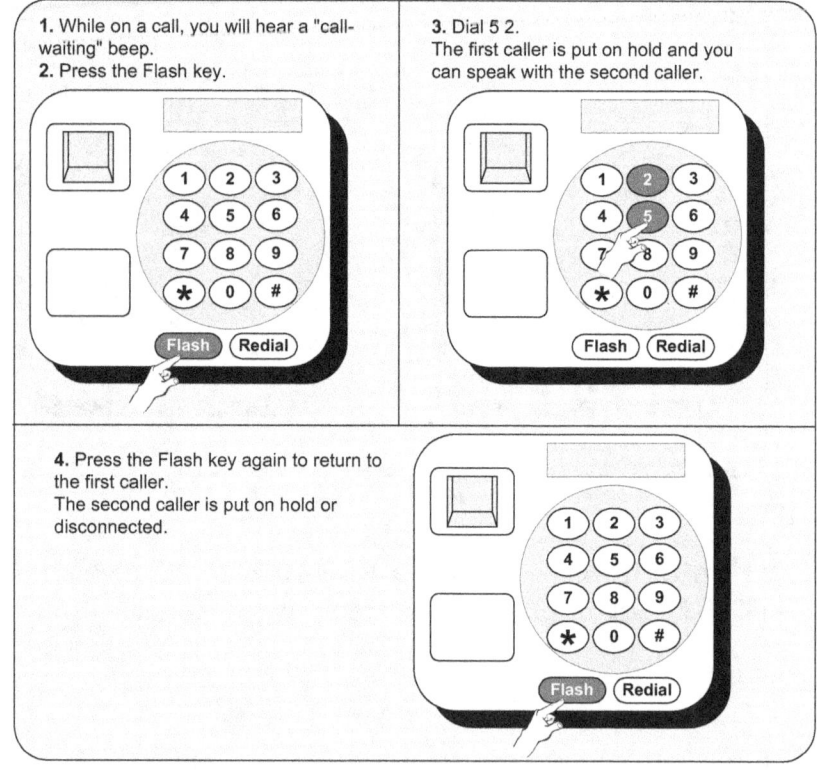

1. While on a call, you will hear a "call-waiting" beep.
2. Press the Flash key.

3. Dial 5 2.
The first caller is put on hold and you can speak with the second caller.

4. Press the Flash key again to return to the first caller.
The second caller is put on hold or disconnected.

Note: If you do not have a Flash Key on your phone, you can still do a Flash by pressing the "Hook-switch" for half a second.

How to Answer an Alternate Ringing Phone

You can answer a call that is ringing at another station extension from an idle station, or when you are on a call.

⇒ From an idle station

1) Lift the receiver.
2) If you hear an inside dial-tone, dial **5 0** to answer the call on the ringing station.
3) If you hear an outside dial-tone, dial *** 5 0** to answer the call on the ringing station. The * switches you to the inside dial-tone.

Note: You may ask why would you get an inside dial-tone sometimes. This happens when all outside CO lines are in use by other extensions. In order to know when you need to dial the * to switch to the inside, it is useful to know the difference between the inside and outside dial-tones. You can compare the difference by simply picking up any extension and listen to the dial-tone. If you have an available line, you are listening to the outside (phone company) dial-tone. Now press the * key and you will hear the inside dial-tone. This is why you need to press the * key before dialing another extension.

⇒ From a station in use

1) Press Flash.
2) Dial **5 0** and you will be switched to the incoming call.
3) Press Flash to return to your original call.

Tip: You can switch back and forth between the two calls using the Flash key.

How to Make Conference Calls

The conference call feature allows you to speak with one outside party and two inside parties, or two outside parties and one inside party.

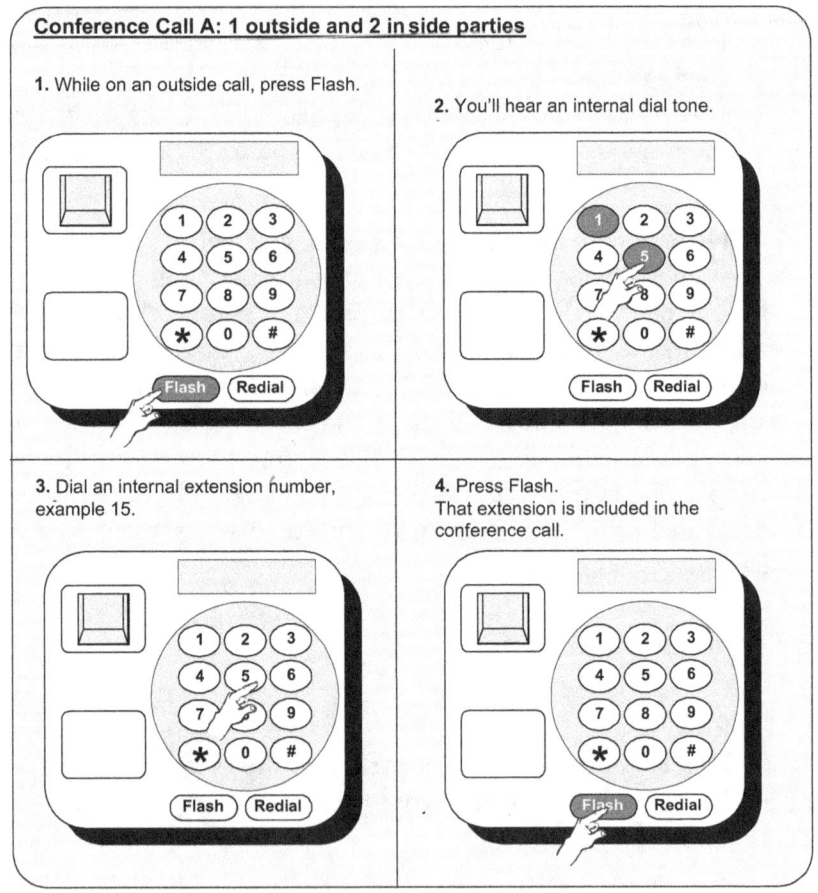

Conference Call A: 1 outside and 2 inside parties

1. While on an outside call, press Flash.

2. You'll hear an internal dial tone.

3. Dial an internal extension number, example 15.

4. Press Flash.
That extension is included in the conference call.

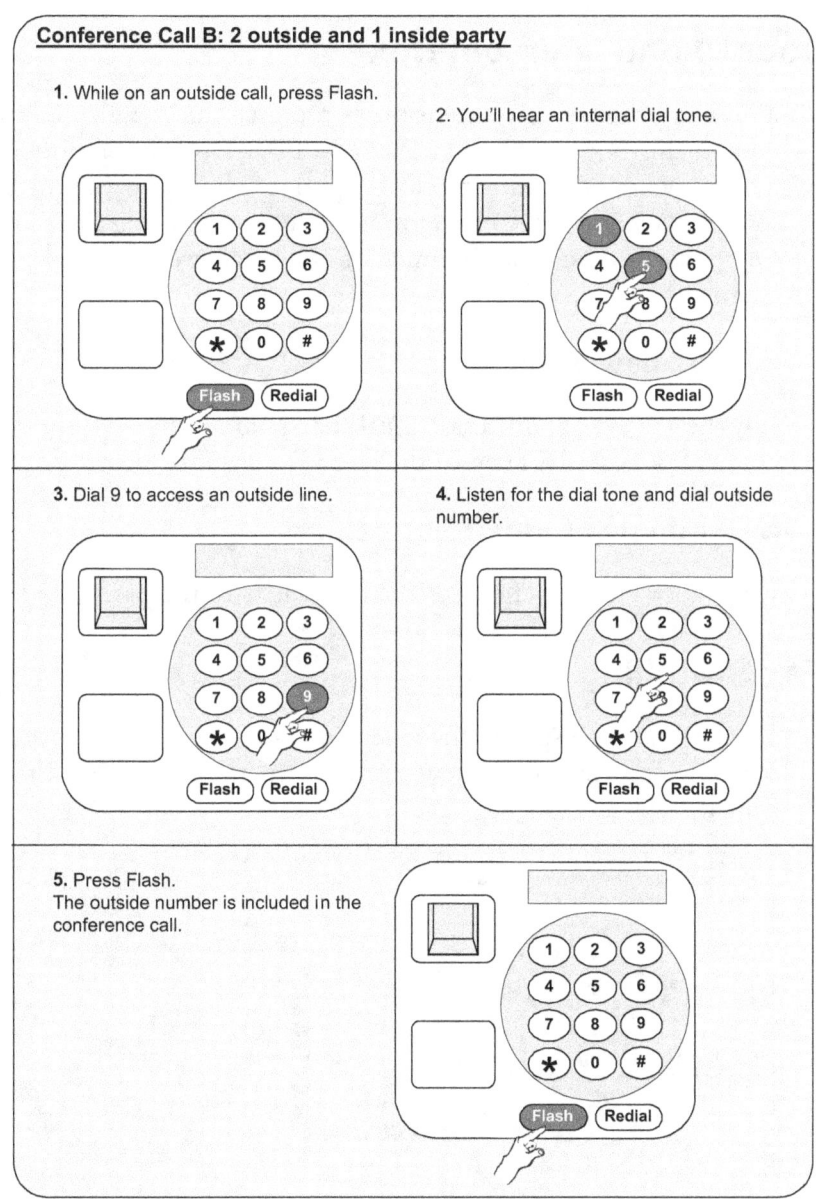

Conference Call B: 2 outside and 1 inside party

1. While on an outside call, press Flash.

2. You'll hear an internal dial tone.

3. Dial 9 to access an outside line.

4. Listen for the dial tone and dial outside number.

5. Press Flash.
The outside number is included in the conference call.

💡 **Tip:** If there are no lines available when you dial 9 to access an outside line, press Flash to return to the original party.

Door Phone Intercom Box

You can program any extension as a door station with the proper equipment (not included) known as a PBX Door Phone Intercom. This functions as an internal telephone extension. See Program Functions 5 and 6 for programming the port and ring assignments. Once installed and programmed, it can be answered like any other extension.

⇒ To answer the door

Lift the receiver and press *. Dial the station number for the door chime. Speak to the guest at the door.

⇒ At door (Hands-free speaking)

Press door chime. When answered, speak with the party.

Fax Switching

You will need to specify the extension where you connect your fax machine and the CO lines where faxes may come in. See Program Functions 7 and 31.

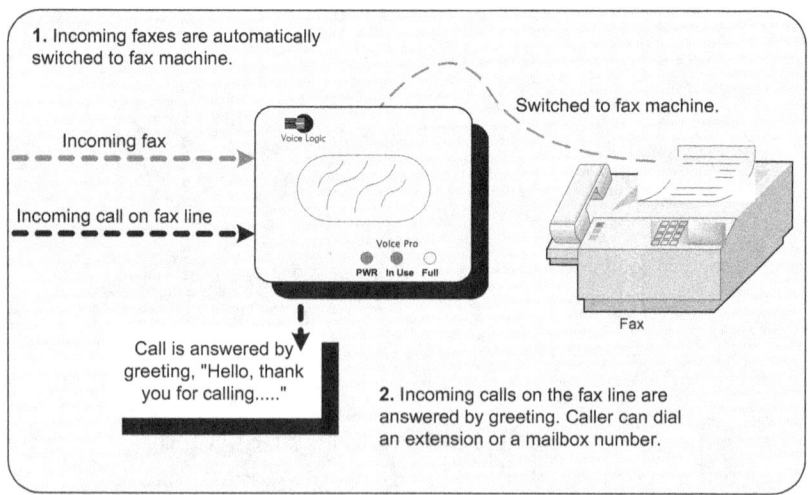

1. Incoming faxes are automatically switched to fax machine.

Switched to fax machine.

Incoming fax

Voice Logic

Incoming call on fax line

Voice Pro

PWR In Use Full

Fax

Call is answered by greeting, "Hello, thank you for calling....."

2. Incoming calls on the fax line are answered by greeting. Caller can dial an extension or a mailbox number.

Placing A Call On Hold

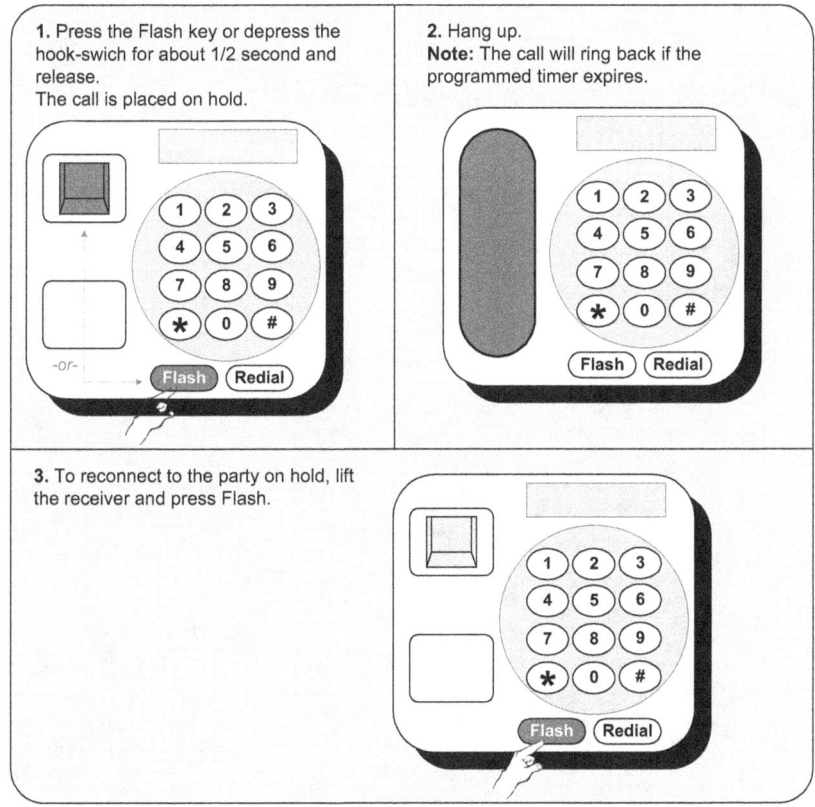

1. Press the Flash key or depress the hook-swich for about 1/2 second and release.
The call is placed on hold.

2. Hang up.
Note: The call will ring back if the programmed timer expires.

3. To reconnect to the party on hold, lift the receiver and press Flash.

Note: Calls that are placed on hold will ring back to its station extension after the programmed hold-timer expires. Valid timeout range is 1 to 999 seconds. The default is 180 seconds. To reconnect to a call ringing back to you, just lift the receiver.

Note: The caller will hear music-on-hold while left on hold if you have a music source connected. Otherwise they will hear silence. This is true when transferring a call as well.

105

Call Screening

You can screen your incoming telephone calls locally or remotely. With simple programming you can enable or disable call-screening mode.

How does call screening work?

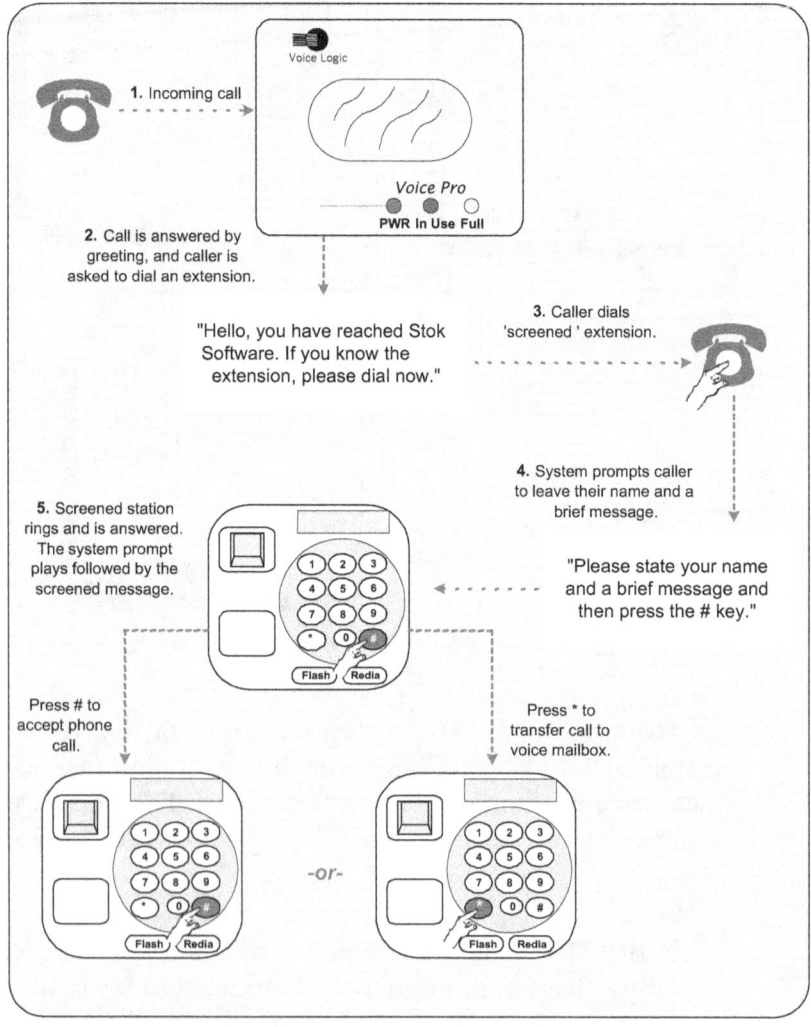

Enable/disable Local Call Screening

1) Lift the receiver.
2) Dial * # for Station Programming.
3) Dial 3 # for extension call screening setup.
4) Do one of the following:
   - To **enable** call screening, dial 1 #.
   - To **disable** call screening, dial 2 #.
5) Dial * * to exit station programming.

Enable Remote Call Screening

1) Lift the receiver.
2) Dial * # for Station Programming.
3) Dial 2 # for remote call screening setup.
4) Enter remote number, followed by #.
5) Dial * * to exit programming.

Disable Remote Call Screening

You can disable remote call screening simply by using the same function. But instead of entering a number, just press #.

1) Lift the receiver.
2) Dial * # for Station Programming.
3) Dial 2 # for remote screening.
4) Press # to disable call screening.
5) Dial * * to exit programming.

Transferring Calls

You can transfer calls to other extensions and announce the party, or just transfer unannounced. Caller will hear music-on-hold while being transferred only if you have a music source connected. You can also transfer a call to a mailbox.

Announced Transfer

1) While talking on an outside line, press Flash.
2) Dial a station extension number when you hear dial tone.
3) When the called party answers, announce the call.
4) Hang up.

Unannounced Transfer

1) While talking on an outside line, press Flash.
2) Dial a station extension number when you hear dial tone.
3) When you hear the ring-through, just hang up.

Transfer to a Mailbox

1) Lift the receiver.
2) Press Flash.
3) Dial mailbox number (3 followed by the extension).
4) Hang up.

Tip: If you receive a busy or ring-no-answer signal, press Flash to return to the caller.

Tip: If you are subscribed to Caller ID service from your phone company, wait for the second ring before picking up in order to capture and transfer caller ID.

Note: When you transfer a call to another extension, the caller ID will be passed to that extension station.

Paging All Extensions

You can ring all idle station extensions at once, except the Fax and door stations, by dialing * 7. This is known as paging.

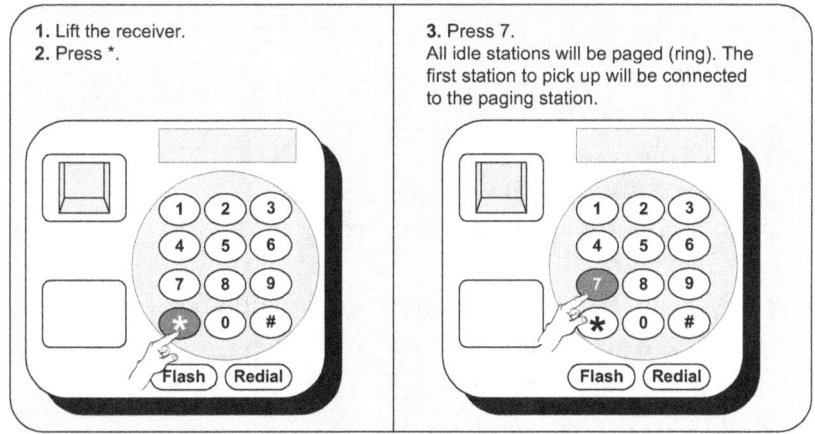

1. Lift the receiver.
2. Press *.

3. Press 7.
All idle stations will be paged (ring). The first station to pick up will be connected to the paging station.

Tip: If you are connected to an outside line when paging, you can transfer the call when it is picked up by another station.

Call Forwarding

You can forward your calls to another station extension, to a voice mailbox, or to another off-site number such as a cell phone. You can also specify to forward all of your calls or just when your extension is busy or ring-no-answer.

Enable/disable Call Forwarding

1) Lift the receiver.
2) Dial * # for Station Programming.
3) Dial 1 # for call forwarding setup.
4) Dial:
   - Another 2-digit station extension number, or
   - A mailbox number (3xx), or
   - An off-site number (toll charges may apply).
5) Press #.
6) Press:
   - 1# to forward all calls, or
   - 2# to forward busy or ring-no-answer calls.
7) Dial * * to exit programming.

To cancel call forwarding

1) Lift the receiver.
2) Dial * # for Station Programming.
3) Dial 1 # # to cancel call forwarding.

▤ **Note:** Call Forwarding only functions for outside callers. If you dial an extension from another station extension, it will ring without regard to the programmed forwarding.

▤ **Note:** You can also set any extension's call forwarding by logging in as the administrator and using Program Function 16.

Extension to Extension Intercom Calls

Intercom calling is just another way of referring to in-house dialing. That is, dialing another extension number from your station.

To place an intercom call

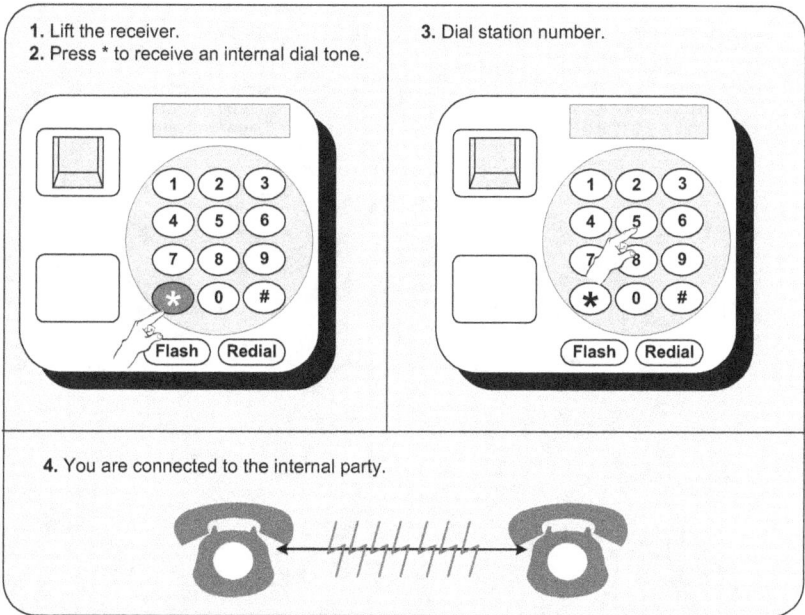

1. Lift the receiver.
2. Press * to receive an internal dial tone.

3. Dial station number.

4. You are connected to the internal party.

To receive an intercom call

- Lift the receiver on the ringing station.

Park and Retrieve a Call

The VoicePro has ten "Parking Orbits" (60 thru 69). These are not considered mailboxes or extensions. You can still use 60 thru 69 as mailboxes.

Parking Orbits are used when you need to move a call from one station to another. You do this by placing the call on hold in a parking orbit. Then you retrieve it at any other extension.

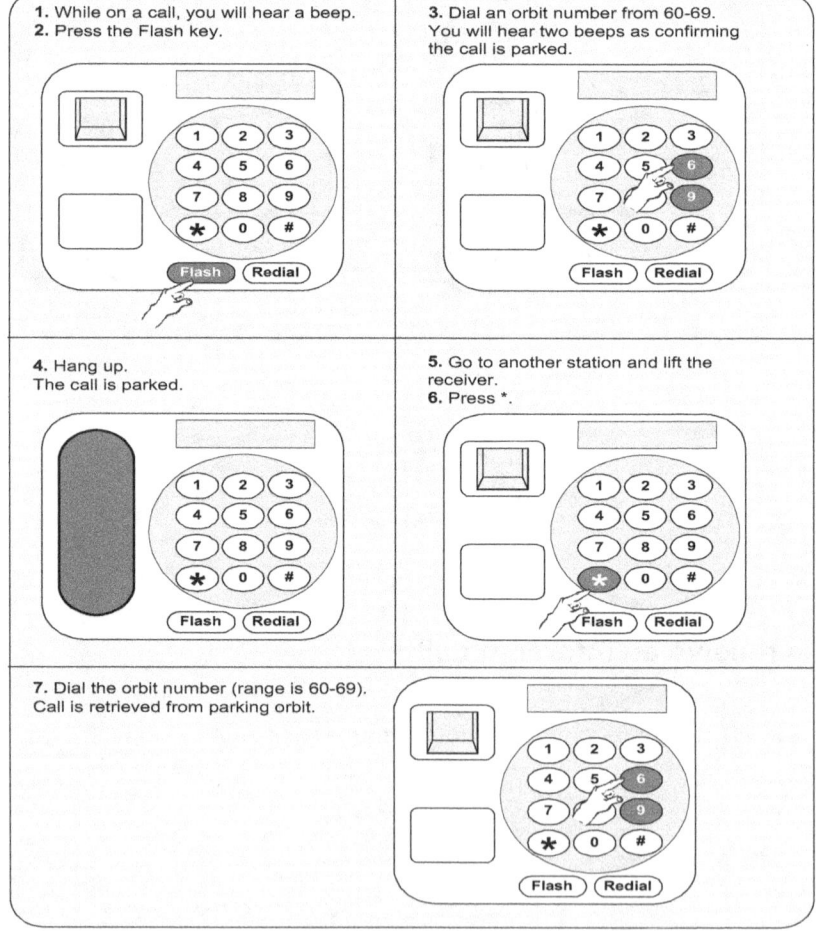

1. While on a call, you will hear a beep.
2. Press the Flash key.

3. Dial an orbit number from 60-69. You will hear two beeps as confirming the call is parked.

4. Hang up. The call is parked.

5. Go to another station and lift the receiver.
6. Press *.

7. Dial the orbit number (range is 60-69). Call is retrieved from parking orbit.

▤ **Note:** If you do not receive a confirmation tone when dialing an orbit number (see step 3 above), then press Flash to retrieve the caller, and repeat the procedure making sure to select an alternate orbit number.

▤ **Note:** A parked call will ring back to its originating station extension if the recall timer expires before it is picked up at another station.

Recording A Conversation

When calls are handled through the VoicePro, you can record a conversation with an outside caller as follows...

To start recording a conversation

1) While talking on an outside line, press Flash.
2) Then press 4.

   The conversation records to your voice mailbox.

To stop recording a conversation

- Press Flash, then 4.
  Or
- Just disconnect the call.

⚡ **Warning:** Recording a conversation without the caller's knowledge may be unlawful in your state.

How to Access Your Mailbox

You can access your voice mailbox locally or remotely. Follow these instructions...

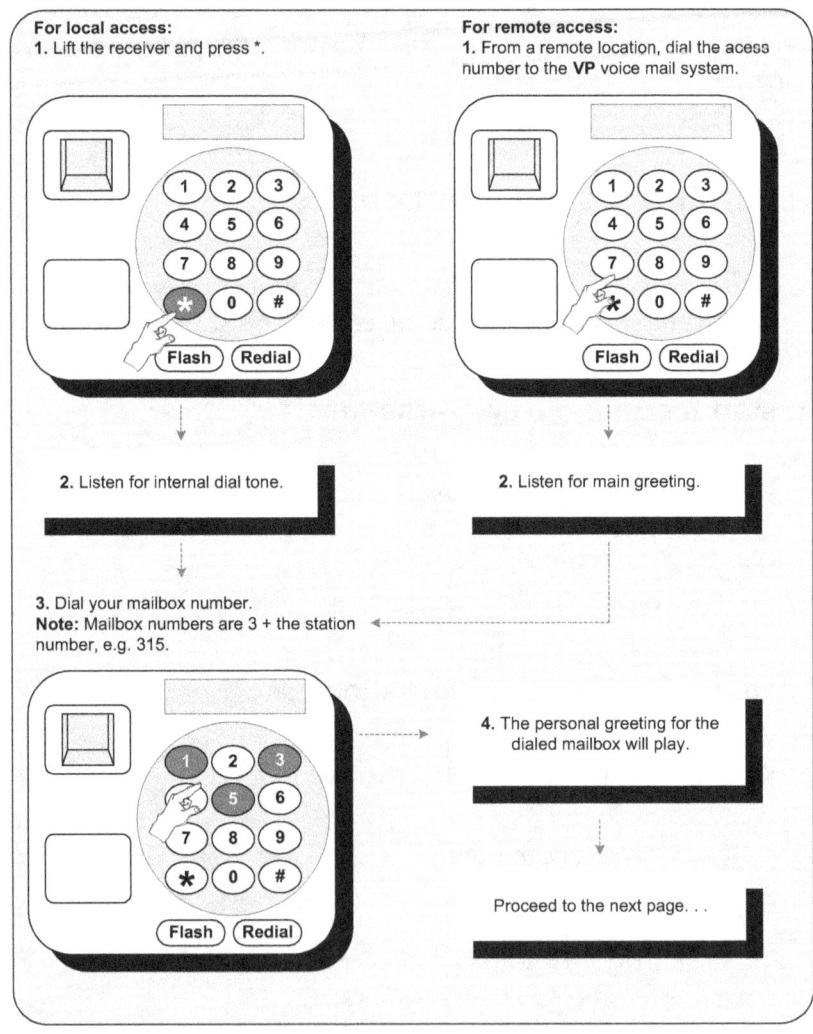

For local access:
1. Lift the receiver and press *.

2. Listen for internal dial tone.

3. Dial your mailbox number.
Note: Mailbox numbers are 3 + the station number, e.g. 315.

For remote access:
1. From a remote location, dial the acess number to the **VP** voice mail system.

2. Listen for main greeting.

4. The personal greeting for the dialed mailbox will play.

Proceed to the next page. . .

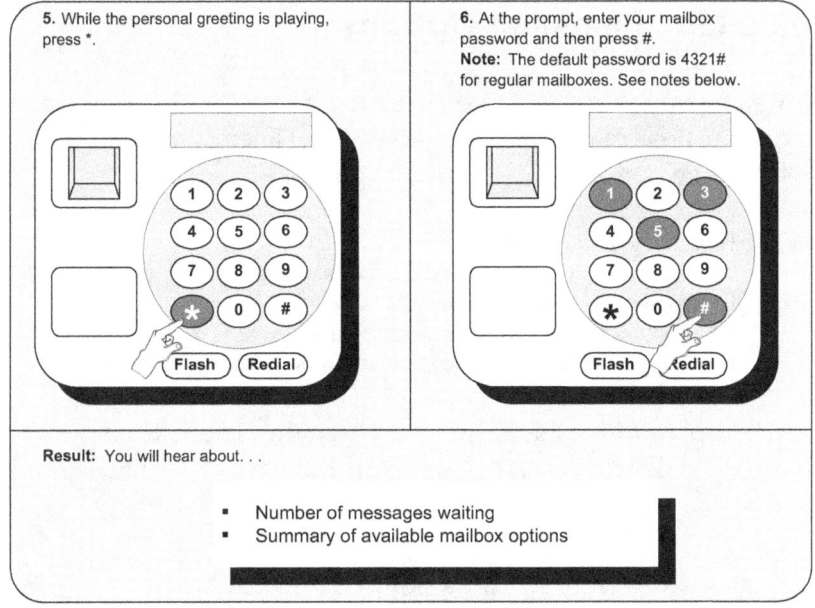

5. While the personal greeting is playing, press *.

6. At the prompt, enter your mailbox password and then press #.
Note: The default password is 4321# for regular mailboxes. See notes below.

Result: You will hear about. . .

- Number of messages waiting
- Summary of available mailbox options

💡 **Tip:** There is a quicker way to log into your own mailbox. Pick up your own extension and dial *300. The system will ask for your password. Dialing *300 works on any extension to log into that extension's mailbox.

📖 **Note:** The default password for Full-featured Mailboxes is 4321#. The default password for Greeting-Only mailboxes is preset to **99.

📖 **Note:** Mailboxes that are assigned to physical extensions default as full-featured. The others are preset as Greeting-Only mailboxes. These mailboxes can be changed to full-featured mailboxes simply by changing the password to one that does not start with a *

Voice Mail Message Options

When you log into your voice mailbox, the VoicePro will announce to you how many messages you have. Then it will announce the following options...

> To play the first message, press 1.
> To undelete previously deleted messages, press 7.
> To program your mailbox, press 9.
> To go to another mailbox, press the star key.
> To hear the options available while listening to messages, press 0.

While playing messages, you will hear the date and time each was recorded. During each message you will have the following options available ...

Option 1: Replay Message

- Press 1 to replay the present message from the beginning.

Option 2: Delete Message

- Press 2 to delete the message.

Option 3: Skip Message

- Press 3 to skip to the next message.

Option 4: Rewind 5 Seconds

- While listening to a message, you can go back five seconds by pressing 4. To keep going back further, just continue pressing 4.

Option 5: Pause/Continue

- Press 5 to pause and press 5 again to continue from where you left off.

Option 6: Go Forward 5 Seconds

- While listening to a message, you can skip forward five seconds at a time by pressing 6. Keep pressing 6 to go further ahead.

Option 7: Reduce Volume

- Press 7 to reduce the volume.
- You can also press 9 to increase the volume.

Option 8: Forward Message to Another Box

- Press 8 to forward the present message to another mailbox. The VoicePro will ask you to enter the mailbox number.

Option 9: Increase the Volume

- Press 9 to increase the volume.

- You can also press 7 to lower the volume.

Your Mailbox Main Menu Options

When you finish playing the last message you will return to the main menu in your mailbox. From there you will have your main options again. Instructions for programming your mailbox begin on the next page.

Option 7: Undelete Messages

- If you did not leave your mailbox, you can undelete previously deleted messages by pressing 7.

Option 9: Program Your Mailbox

- Press 9 to program your mailbox: Change your password, record a greeting, and set "Message Alert."

Option 0: Play Instructions

- Press 0 to hear the options available while listening to messages.

Option *: Go To Another Mailbox

- Press the * key to go to another mailbox.
- At the prompt, enter the 2-digit mailbox number.

How to Program Your Mailbox

You can program your mailbox by logging into it (See page 114) and pressing option 9. Then you can do the following:

1. Change your password
2. Record your personal greeting
3. Program a Message Alert

Change your password

While logged into your mailbox, press 9 and then...

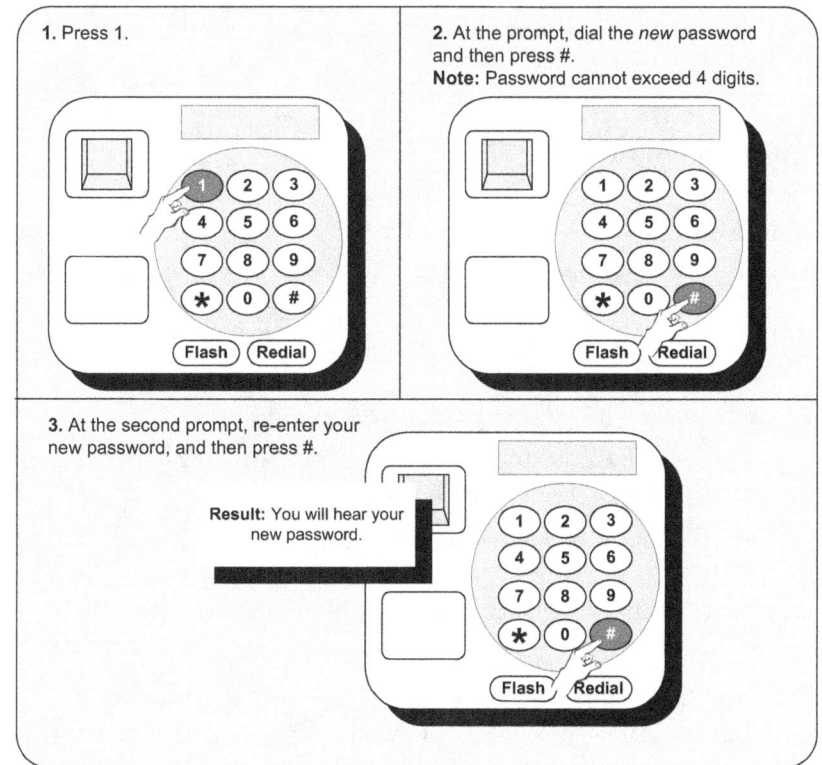

1. Press 1.

2. At the prompt, dial the *new* password and then press #.
Note: Password cannot exceed 4 digits.

3. At the second prompt, re-enter your new password, and then press #.

Result: You will hear your new password.

119

Record your personal greeting

While logged into your mailbox, press 9 and then...

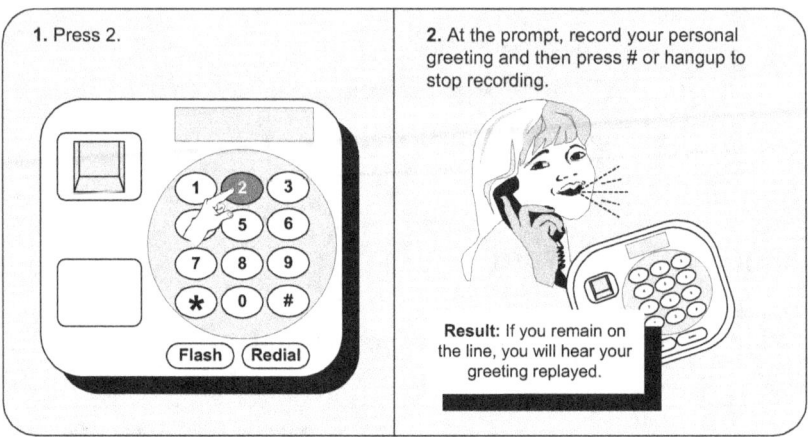

1. Press 2.

2. At the prompt, record your personal greeting and then press # or hangup to stop recording.

Result: If you remain on the line, you will hear your greeting replayed.

Program a "Message Alert"

The VoicePro has two methods of alerting you that you have messages in any mailbox...Pager Alert and Live Message Alert.

While logged into your mailbox, press 9 and then...

- Press 3 for Message Alert programming.
- Press 1 to program Live Telephone Message Alert
- OR Press 2 to program pager alert.
- Continue by following the prompts.

See page 56 and 57 for programming details of both methods.

Note: When using Pager Alert and you do not call in to pick up your messages, a second page will be dispatched if the first page is not responded to within 15 minutes.

120

Examples of Message Alert Pager Entries

Standard Pager:

```
Pager Number       Code to Display    Complete
999-999-9999  *         99               #
```

SkyPager:

```
Pager Access      Pager Number    Code to Display    Complete
999-999-9999 * 999-999-9999 *          99               #
```

Note: Do not include " - " in the phone numbers. The * is used as a separator between fields to insert a 2-second delay. The "code to display" is whatever you want to indicate to you that you have a message in your VoicePro mailbox. The # is the terminator to complete the programming.

Tip: The asterisk (*) inserts a 2-second delay. You may include more asterisks to extend the delay time as needed.

Disable "Message Alert"

1. Log into your mailbox (See page 114)
2. Press Mailbox Option 9 to program.
3. Press Mailbox Option 3 to select Message Alerts.
4. Press Mailbox Option 3 again to disable Message Alerts.
5. You will hear "Message alert is disabled."

Caller Options

When a caller phones in to your VoicePro system, they can:

- Direct dial a 2-digit extension (nn).
- Select Auto Attendant Menu Options (0 thru 99)
- Request the phone directory (option 9).
- Dial into a voice mailbox and leave a message (3nn).

Direct Dial an Extension

While the greeting is playing, dial the two-digit extension of the party they wish to reach. The call is transferred to that extension. The system can be programmed to transfer unanswered calls to the station's mailbox to take a message.

Select Auto Attendant Menu Key Option

If you have programmed a custom Auto Attendant menu and recorded prompts in a menu greeting for your caller to hear, then they can select any menu option you had programmed by dialing its Menu Key (anything from 0 to 99). Dialing " 0 " rings to the phone you have connected as extension 10.

Request Phone Directory

While the greeting is playing, press 9 to hear the phone directory. The prerecorded directory is played for the caller. This is actually greeting number 9 and can be recorded with Program Function 25.

Dial Into a Voice Mailbox and Leave a Message

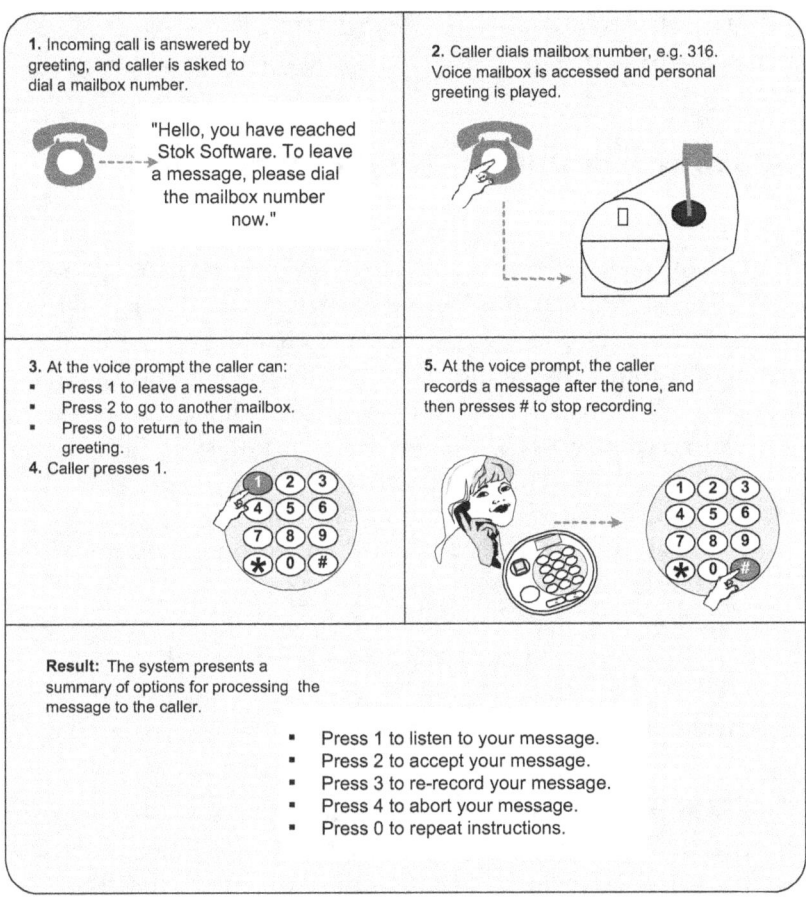

1. Incoming call is answered by greeting, and caller is asked to dial a mailbox number.

"Hello, you have reached Stok Software. To leave a message, please dial the mailbox number now."

2. Caller dials mailbox number, e.g. 316. Voice mailbox is accessed and personal greeting is played.

3. At the voice prompt the caller can:
- Press 1 to leave a message.
- Press 2 to go to another mailbox.
- Press 0 to return to the main greeting.

4. Caller presses 1.

5. At the voice prompt, the caller records a message after the tone, and then presses # to stop recording.

Result: The system presents a summary of options for processing the message to the caller.

- Press 1 to listen to your message.
- Press 2 to accept your message.
- Press 3 to re-record your message.
- Press 4 to abort your message.
- Press 0 to repeat instructions.

You can also dial into a voice mailbox to leave a message from any internal extension...

1. Lift the receiver and press * for the internal dial tone.
2. Enter 3 followed by the mailbox number (301 thru 399).
3. While the personal greeting is playing, press 1 to leave a message.

Only regular voice mailboxes will accept messages. If a mailbox has a password that starts with a *, then it is a greeting-only mailbox. Passwords can be changed to designate mailboxes to be full featured of greeting-only. A password that starts with a star forces a mailbox to only play its greeting without taking a message.

Accessing Telephone Company Features

When you pick up any extension the VoicePro gives you outside dialtone. If you press the * key then you get inside dialtone so that you can dial another extension. But what if you want to access telephone company features such as ***69** to hear and call back the last caller. Many local telephone companies make use of the * and # keys. To gain access to these types of features, do the following:

1. Lift the receiver on your extension.
2. Dial * * and listen for outside dial tone (You may need to pause a second between the two stars).
3. Now you can dial the code for the feature you want and the * or # will not interfere with the VoicePro.

Example: To access the *69 feature, dial * pause * pause * 6 9.

Call Waiting is another feature that requires you to bypass the VoicePro. When you hear a Call Waiting Tone the usual way to take that call is to do a "Flash." But if you press the flash button the VoicePro will put you on hold and give you another dialtone. This is a function of the VoicePro used to make conference calls.

You need to be able to do a "Flash" on the outside line when you hear a Call Waiting Tone. You can do this by dialing **5 2** after pressing the Flash Key on your phone.

Sample System Prompts

Default Main Greeting (Greeting 0)

"Thank you for calling. If you know your party's number, please enter it now. Otherwise for a directory, press 9. Or for an operator, press zero."

📖 **Note:** This is the default greeting that is played for all other greetings 1 thru 99 unless any of 1 thru 99 has been changed.

Default Name Directory (Greeting 9)

"The directory is not available."

📖 **Note:** This is what plays when a caller presses 9. You may customize this recording by using Function 25.

Undefined menu option selected by caller

"Your call cannot be completed as dialed. Please try again."

Live Message Alert

"This is a voice notification from VoicePro. You have a message in mailbox 10. Please enter your mailbox password."

Call Screening Prompt

"Please record your name and a short message at the tone."

📖 **Note:** You may customize this prompt by using Function 32.

Mailbox Login

"Please enter your mailbox password followed by the pound or press pound to go to another mailbox."

Mailbox Options

"You have 1 new message and 2 saved messages. To play the first message, press 1. To undelete all previously deleted messages, press 7. To program your voice mailbox, press 9. To hear options that are available while listening to messages, press zero. To go to another mailbox, press the star key."

Programming Mode Login

"Welcome to VoicePro. Please enter your password followed by the pound. You may exit the program mode at any time by entering star star (* *)."

Programming Mode Confirmation

"Password accepted. Please enter the program number, followed by the pound."

Extension Station Programming

"Welcome to Station Programming. For call forwarding set up press 1 plus pound. For remote call screening setup press 2 plus pound. For extension call screening setup press 3 plus pound."

Registration Information

The VoicePro has been registered with the Federal Communications Commission (FCC). It meets FCC requirements and may be connected directly to your telephone line. On the bottom of this equipment is a label that contains, among other information, the FCC registration number and Ringer Equivalence Number (REN) for this equipment. If requested, this information must be provided to the telephone company representative. Use the REN to help determine the maximum number of devices you can connect to your telephone without eliminating their ability to ring when your number is called. In many areas, the sum of RENs of all devices connected to one line should not exceed 5.0. To determine how many devices you can connect to your line, contact your local telephone company to find out the maximum REN for your area.

The VoicePro may not be connected to a party line or coin line telephone network. If the VoicePro does not function properly, disconnect the unit. If the VoicePro causes harm to the network, the phone company may discontinue your service temporarily. If possible, they will notify you in advance. But if advance notice is not practical, the phone company will notify you as soon as possible. You will be advised of your right to file a complaint with the FCC if you believe it is necessary.

To order a modular jack from the phone company, request a USOCRJ11C or a USOCRJ13C.

FCC Rules Part 15 - Computing Devices

This equipment has been tested and found to comply with the limits for a Class B digital device, pursuant to Part 15 of the FCC rules. These limits are designed to provide reasonable protection against harmful interference in a residential installation. This equipment generates, uses, and can radiate radio frequency energy and, if not installed and used in accordance with the instructions, may cause harmful interference to radio communications. However, there is no guarantee that interference will not occur in a particular installation. If this equipment does cause harmful interference to radio or television reception, which can be determined by turning the equipment off and on, the user is encouraged to try to correct the interference by one or more of the following measures:

- Reorient or relocate the receiving antenna.
- Increase the separation between the equipment and receiver.
- Connect the VoicePro into an outlet on a different circuit from the receiver.
- Consult the dealer or an experienced radio/TV technician for help.

Canada Users

This Class B digital apparatus meets all requirements of the Canadian Interference-Causing Equipment Regulations.

Cet appareil numérique de la classe B respecte toutes les exigences du Règlement sur le matériel brouilleur du Canada.

Notice: The Industry Canada (IC) label identifies Certified Equipment. This certification means that the equipment meets certain telecommunications network protective, operational, and safety retirements as prescribed in the appropriate Terminal Equipment Technical Requirements documents. The Department does not guarantee the equipment will operate to the user's satisfaction.

Before installing this equipment, users should ensure that it is permissible to be connected to the facilities of the local Telecommunications Company. The equipment must also be installed using an acceptable method of connection. The customer should be aware that compliance with the above conditions might not prevent degradation of service in some situations.

A representative designated by the supplier should coordinate repairs to Certified equipment. Any repairs or alterations made by the user to this equipment, or equipment malfunctions, may give the Telecommunications Company cause to request the user to disconnect the equipment.

Users should ensure, for their own protection, that the electrical ground connections of the power utility, telephone lines, and internal metallic water pipe system, if present, are all connected together. This precaution may be particularly important in rural areas.

Important: Users should not attempt to make such connections themselves, but should contact the appropriate electric inspection authority, or an electrician, as appropriate.

The Ringer Equivalent Number (REN) assigned to each terminal device provides an indication of the maximum number of terminals allowed to be connected to a telephone interface. The termination of an interface may consist of any combination of devices subject only to the retirement that the sum of the Ringer Equivalence Numbers of all the devices does not exceed five (5).